TRAUMA:

Time, Space and Fractals

Anngwyn St. Just

TRAUMA: TIME, SPACE and FRACTALS

Also by Anngwyn St. Just

A Question of Balance:
A Systemic Approach to Understanding and Resolving Trauma
2009, Createspace

Relative Balance in an Unstable World:
A Search for New Models for Trauma Education and Recovery
2006, Carl Auer

In Translation:

Equilibrio relativo en un mundo inestable.
Una investigación sobre Educación de Traumas y Recuperación.
Ed. Alma Lepik, Buenos Aires / Argentina

Soziales Trauma.
Balance finden in einer unsicheren Welt
Kösel Verlag/Random House München, 2005

Trauma: una cuestión de equilibrio
Un abordaje sistémico para la comprensión y resolución
Ed. Alma Lepik, Buenos Aires / Argentina

Copyright © 2012 Anngwyn St. Just

All rights reserved.

ISBN: 1477459723

ISBN-13: 978-1477459720

TRAUMA: TIME, SPACE and FRACTALS

TABLE OF CONTENTS

Introduction	1
1. Calendars, Consciousness and Control	13
2. Checking the Time	34
3. The Replicating Fractal of Katyn	53
4. Japan: Land of the Setting Sun	77
5. Fukushima Daiichi Complex	99
6. The Crane	126
7. Blind Spot	138
8. The Nuclear Family	153
9. Our House Divided	173
10. Tree of Liberty	190
11. Old Myths and Remembered Glories	205
Conclusion	226
Appendix	233
Notes	235
Bibliography	244

TRAUMA: TIME, SPACE and FRACTALS

For my mother

Gwendolyn Ruth Thomas.......

TRAUMA: TIME, SPACE and FRACTALS

"For people like us, who believe in physics, know that the distinction between past, present and future is only a stubbornly persistent illusion".

Albert Einstein

TRAUMA: TIME, SPACE and FRACTALS

INTRODUCTION

Fractals have been called the "fingerprints of God"

(Arthur C. Clarke: The Colors of Infinity)

My first book, *Relative Balance in an Unstable World: A Search for New Models of Trauma Education and Recovery* described a challenging process of moving beyond a medical-surgical understanding of the kinds of shock and trauma that manifested on a physiological level. Eventually, I was able to evolve toward an expanded view of trauma which included multiple body-mind components of overwhelming life experiences. In time, I also came to a realization that it is vitally important to seek an understanding of the many social, cultural, political and religious dimensions inherent within any experience of trauma. These powerful external forces extend, not only into family, community, and nations, but further still on into our biosphere and the environmental totality of our planetary home. My second book, *A Question of*

TRAUMA: TIME, SPACE and FRACTALS

Balance: A Systemic Approach to Understanding and Resolving Trauma continues this process of expansion. It draws attention to a wide range of contextual factors that contribute to overwhelming life events such as synchronicity, anniversary dates, history of place, family dynamics, cross cultural and other societal elements. From this newly discovered systemic perspective, I found that a healing process often involves a recognition of a need for interconnectedness and balance in order to draw strength and meaning from adversity. In this sense, one could say that my second effort sets forth a therapeutic approach that is as much a world view as it is a method.

Now, with *Trauma: Space, Time and Fractals,* I have turned to a deeper exploration into the role of time in my ongoing effort to understand the causes, experience and healing of individual, social and global trauma. Physicists are now telling us that the Universe and time itself are composed of an infinite series of expanding and contracting cycles within cycles. This new version of reality conjures images of vast cosmic cycles mirrored in smaller scales of planetary cycles, human civilizations, community and family systems, as well as individual lives. Each life is lived within a cycle which is lived as an integral fragment of other cycles nested within increasingly larger cycles. These larger cycles contain smaller cycles and still smaller cycles because they contain universal fractal patterns which repeat themselves in non-linear self-similar ways as described in the axiom, "As above, so below". In many traditions, some, if not all of these hidden designs are recognized as fate.

The natural environment that we live in is based upon fractal geometric designs; trees, branches, river deltas, spiraling vines, sea shells and so on. For those willing to see, fractals are absolutely everywhere, on land and sea, and clearly evident throughout our day and night skies. Self-similar patterns can be seen through microscopes and

TRAUMA: TIME, SPACE and FRACTALS

telescopes. Fractal designs repeat throughout our human bodily organs, as we can see in the cochlear spirals of our ear canals, and tissues bearing branching patterns of blood vessels and intricate neural networks. A fractal vision of trauma therefore, sees our individual human experiences, relationships and families as part of a much greater whole which includes Nature, culture and historical context. At this point in my understanding, fractal-like iterations of similar underlying dynamics, evident within individual and collective experiences of trauma, seem to be generated by something like a tension between lack of resolution, will to completion and... fate.

In work with trauma one encounters at least two kinds of time, *chronos* determined by linear measurements of clock and calendar and *cheiros* which is extremely subjective. Also known as sacred or dream time, *cheiros* can be experienced as radically altered time, speeding up or slowing down, or even standing still in times of crisis, meditation, revelation and dreams. While this phenomenon is well known within a variety of approaches to resolving individual trauma, the role of time in an understanding of social trauma in realms of community, nation and environmental matrices has received little attention. Cross cultural issues in the understanding of time became an area of special interest as I began working with many layers of social trauma throughout Latin America. Eventually, this new area of interest became a topic of my initial chapter; Calendar, Consciousness and Control. The arrival of European conquerors along the shores of this New World, delivered a near-fatal shock to existing social orders of that era. As has been true throughout history, conquerors invoke the "right of might" to impose their own calendars and understanding of time. Those in control of the cultural calendar always have the power to tell all others, "what time it is". European Catholics brought along their strict, linear, Earthbound, commercial, Gregorian calendar which stood in radical contrast to ancient, nature oriented rhythms of indigenous daily life. This collision of cultures resulted in a *crisis of perception* in their vastly different understanding of time, space and the nature of the Universe. As the Europeans gained almost complete control, the few remaining Time Keepers withdrew into obscurity in hopes of preserving at least a few of their indigenous traditions.

One of the most important of these traditions was their Pre-Colombian calendar. This highly sophisticated time keeping system reached a highpoint with the Maya. Their calendar consisted of a non-linear system of interlocking almanacs with computer-like circuitry, reflecting a fractal Universe wherein each part is a reflection of the whole. The recent re-emergence of the Mayan calendar into modern consciousness is of particular interest in relation to our own understanding, both of the nature of time, and our own place within a fractal Universe.

TRAUMA: TIME, SPACE and FRACTALS

Since we now know that calendars and other time keeping devices are culturally determined and valid only on this planet, one might be led to wonder "What time is it really?" "Checking the Time", then became the subject for Chapter Two. As we transitioned from the Twentieth into the Twenty First century, the arrival of a new millennium brought forth predictable fears that an end of a century could also mean an end of the world. This linear understanding of *chronos*, held by several major religions, pre-supposes both a beginning and an end to time. A number of earlier civilizations understood a deeper truth, as did the Maya. *Chronos* may be linear, but time is not. The Maya understood *Cheiros,* ceremonial or dream time, and also as we now know, that the nature of time is fractal. Within these definitions of time are also patterns which repeat in self-similar ways on different scales, in different time frames, places and subsequent generations. Herein may also lie an explanation of the complex relationship between humans and time.

TRAUMA: TIME, SPACE and FRACTALS

Within mysteries of deep time and the cosmos, those who care to look will find resonance throughout patterns of history, as well as in our individual and family lives. While this fractal reality may appear to be too abstract for many of us who work with trauma, it is a fact that overwhelming life events can affect the way both the individual and the collective consciousness experience time. In this second chapter one can begin to see that underlying the seeming chaos of traumatic events, self-similar, repetitive patterns remain as an indication of that which is in need of resolution. These fractal patterns may also manifest through many layers of complex social systems. A closer look at non-linear repetition and anniversary dynamics in larger social and political systems takes place in Chapter Three: Katyn. Here the focus is upon the mysteries surrounding the April 10, 2010 Polish plane crash in the Russian village of Katyn. There is much to ponder in view of the previous history of that date, that place and the identity of those who died, as well as the predictable aftermath of cover-ups and lies.

In Chapter Four, Japan: Land of the Setting Sun, traumatic patterns repeat in a series of uncanny collective flashbacks to the atomic horrors of World War II. Their nuclear disaster in Fukushima, which has been called "the third atomic bombing of Japan", cannot be understood apart from the country's relationship with the USA and our shared obsession with nuclear power. This greatest nuclear catastrophe since Chernobyl may have rendered Japan uninhabitable and seriously poisoned the rest of our homeworld.

Chapter Five involves an overview of the current situation at the Fukushima Daiichi Complex and the likely trajectory for future events. With a massive social trauma as dire as what is now taking place in Japan, one wonders how this population can best respond to yet another, more severe, nuclear devastation. This question of what heals and what helps became the focus of Chapter

TRAUMA: TIME, SPACE and FRACTALS

Six: The Crane. When I began this project, I was not sufficiently aware of the degree to which individual, family, social and environmental trauma has been inflicted by massive amounts of radiation unleashed since the dawn of the Atomic Age. Adding to this still unfolding nightmare we find an official policy of denial by those responsible who insist that they have neither personal nor political accountability. Once I realized that this nuclear genii was out of the bottle, the material continued to mushroom. As is its nature, the subject of the bomb and the power plants, two fruits of the same tree, demanded ever more space and the need for more research than I had initially foreseen. It soon became evident that I could easily write an entire volume on the subject of trauma and radiation. Perhaps I will undertake that challenge sometime in the near future, if indeed we actually have one. For now however, in addition to the material devoted to the Japanese disaster, Chapters Seven and Eight address my concern for what might be understood as nuclear trauma.

Chapters Nine and Ten take up a discussion of current events here in the USA which appear to be seriously entangled with previous events having to do with state's rights, slavery and racism. The occasion of the 150th commemoration of our Civil War between the Northern Union and Southern Confederacy, with a Black man in the White House, has brought to light a bevy of unresolved tensions. It was fervently hoped by many that with the advent of this historic Obama presidency, the ugly ambitions of our White Supremacists would finally recede. Unfortunately, the exact opposite has proven to be the case. We now find ourselves facing a cultural divide eerily similar to that which preceded the Civil War. Overt racism has re-surfaced and threats of secession are in the air. Only time will tell how these volatile and self-replicating trends will unfold. One can always hope that these endless loops of traumatic re-enactment and other repetitive historical and trans-generational traumas can be avoided. I look forward to time when the good people of America and other troubled nations find a way to open their hearts and minds to something new.

Anngwyn St. Just, November 2011

TRAUMA: TIME, SPACE and FRACTALS

1

CALENDARS, CONSCIOUSNESS AND CONTROL

Calendars are subliminal programming devices orienting us to a particular perspective on time, space and being.

(Ian Xel Lungold)

While social trauma is endemic throughout our world, this topic is especially relevant to an understanding of Central and South American history and culture. When I was invited to offer seminars and trauma training programs in several of these southern countries, an inevitable series of cross cultural challenges opened a way toward a deepening appreciation of Latin American complexities. Until then, most of my historical studies had focused on the United States, Europe and Russia and there was still much to learn about our neighbors to the South. The cultural history of the Latin American continent reveals vast and diverse regions with many layers of unresolved trauma. Beginning in Pre-Colombian times, various populations endured multiple wars, slavery, torture, human sacrifice, famine, epidemics and natural disasters. Without exception, these countries have experienced overwhelming interventions and exploitations of colonial rule resulting in many residual and reverberating collective traumas. In turn, these unresolved social traumas have led to more wars, revolutions and economic and other forms of exploitation, which continue to this day. Much of this ongoing trauma is carefully documented in Eduardo Galleano's, now classic, *The Open Veins of Latin America*.

The arrival of Conquistadores along the shores of the "New World" was an enormous shock to existing social orders of that time. Soon to follow were European missionaries and their insistence upon an immediate imposition of European values, and a particularly cruel version of Catholic Christianity. These newcomers also imposed the strict linear discipline of their Gregorian calendar which presented a *radically* different time frame from ancient, nature oriented rhythms of indigenous daily life. As has been the case throughout human history, along with language, religion, and currency, conquerors impose both their own calendars and a right to determine and decree their own understanding of time. All calendars represent subliminal chronological devices designed to orient entire populations to a particular perspective on time, space and being and therefore represent very effective tools of control. While in a positive sense, calendars can also serve as a means of unification and joining of people together in a common understanding of time, there remains a potential for abuse when *chronos* is employed as a means to further prejudice, suffering and chaos.

Culturally determined calendars represent macro-organizing principles and an absolute center point for the consciousness of any civilization. If one defines consciousness as "the awareness of being aware", then you become aware of that to which you pay attention. Free will is the choice of where and to what you will or won't place your attention. In controlled societies of the conquered, new authorities decide how and where their subjects need to direct their attention and this also means the right to tell them "what time it is".[1]

The Conquistadors brought along their European, Catholic calendar imposed by Pope Gregory XIII and his Council of Trent in a Papal Bull in 1582, "Year of our Lord". This new calendar was compiled as a correction for inaccuracies in the old Roman calendar inaugurated by Julius Caesar in 46 BC. It is interesting to note that the word calendar is derived from the Latin meaning of "account book" and this Julian calendar was imposed to facilitate a Roman system of tax collection. Here we also find the origin of the still familiar concept "time is money", which persisted until the Industrial Revolution and continues on in all materialist cultures characterized by exploitation and greed.

TRAUMA: TIME, SPACE and FRACTALS

Pope Gregory's revised calendar was a Christian Catholic device organized around canonical and liturgical festivities and included new rules for determining dates for Easter. In Western Europe, most Catholic countries readily complied. There soon appeared, however, a considerable resistance to this new time frame in other parts of the Old World. In the city of Frankfurt, violent protests broke out against this Pope and his mathematicians by people who feared that their lives would now be shortened by 10 days.

Pious worshippers worried that their prayers would not be heard if they were offered ten days later than traditional dates for honoring each saint's day. Unmoved by threats of ex-communication, other countries embroiled in their versions of a Protestant Reformation saw this as a ploy to return them to a Catholic fold. There were "calendar riots" in Riga in 1584 and bloody uprisings, such as those in Staemark and Ausberg which led to a disastrous Thirty Years War (1618-1648). Eastern Orthodox territories also resisted, mostly for reasons having to do with differences in religious doctrine, as well as the fact that much of Central and Eastern Europe remained under Muslim domination until the collapse of the Ottoman Empire during the First World War.[2]

Over in the New World, immediate and ongoing resistance of indigenous cultures to their conqueror's calendar had more to do with a "crisis of perception" and fundamental difference in their understanding of time, space and the nature of the Universe. While the exact origin of Mesoamerican calendars in use at the time of the Conquistadors remains speculative, archeological evidence points to an enigmatic Olmec settlement of uncertain origin located in Izapa in southeastern Chiapas, Mexico circa 1200 BC. This calendar was in use during the Pre-Classic Maya era (2000 BC -250 A.D) and then it was extended and refined during Classic Maya civilization (250 – 900 A.D.) and later adapted by Aztec and several other Pre-Colombian cultures.[3]

The Maya were and are an agriculturally intense, Native American people living in what is now Guatemala, El Salvador, Western Honduras, Northern Belize and Southern Mexico. Their advanced culture emerged around the time of the early Roman Empire. By the third century BC, independent city states and temple sites proliferated throughout Central America until a time of collapse early in the ninth century A.D., for reasons unknown and still under debate.

This enigmatic civilization produced brilliant mathematicians, astronomers, artists, temple builders and city planners. The Maya were also the only Pre-Columbian people to have a fully developed written language. In contrast to our Earth bound, linear Gregorian model which is limited to a physical measurement of cycles of our sun and moon, the more cosmic calculations of the Maya Day Keepers expanded to include cycles of other planets, along with their Venus calendar of 584 days. Some scholars such as Carl Johan Calleman believe calculations of the Maya time line extends from 16.4 billion years ago. This is the date believed to mark the beginning of the Universe discovered on Tortuguero Monument 6.[4]

One could envision the Maya calendar as a non-linear system of interlocking almanacs with a computer-like circuitry reflecting a fractal universe wherein each part is a reflection of the whole. Classic Maya employed three main calendric systems, intermeshed like different size cogs on a wheel; the *Tzolkin, Haab and Baktun*. The *Tzolkin* consists of glyphs and binary patterns. Those depicting a personal and sacred or 260 day ceremonial cycle also mark birth dates and day names for divination, determination of life purpose, and personality traits, much like astrological signs today. This calendar is composed of 20 day signs in thirteen combinations, measuring agricultural, astronomical, and human cycles. These cycles also corresponded to appearances and conjunctions of the planet Venus as both Morning and Evening Stars, as well as the gestation period of the human embryo.

The *Tzolkin* also served as a kind of Farmer's Almanac used to guide the growth cycle of maize, and determine the most auspicious days for planting and harvest. And, because of its association with seeds and fertility it has been speculated that this daily *Tzolkin* was also used in predictive family planning. Time Keeper priests and other members of the ruling classes who possessed knowledge of this and other calendars were in a strong position to obtain and maintain complete control over the general populace.

The Maya *Haab* is a 365 day civil calendar, with 360 days plus five extra days at the end of every year, as a transition period between cycles. These 5 days, known as *wayeb,* were considered to be unlucky and a time of danger when gods rested and left Earth unprotected. Together, their daily sacred

TRAUMA: TIME, SPACE and FRACTALS

Tzolkin and civil *Haab* comprise a Calendar Round, the first large cycle of the Maya timekeeping system. Every 52 years, dates from these two calendars match up and this conjunction inaugurates another cycle. This Calendar Round was the longest time period calculated by Aztecs and other Mesoamerican people. Only Maya and their Olmec predecessors calculated and observed longer counts. Their current long count cycle of thirteen 394 year-long *baktuns* which began on August 11, 3114 BC is believed by many to end a Great Cycle on December 21, 2012, thus completing our Age of the Jaguar and their Five Worlds calendar.[5]

In *The 2012 Story,* John Major Jenkins states his belief that this date signals an end of an even larger cycle – a *precessional year* that began 25,920 years ago when Earth began a celestial journey around the wheel of the zodiac. This, he also believes, is a date when our solar system will move across the galactic equator into a projected alignment with the absolute center of our Milky Way Galaxy. The meaning of this event for life on Earth has been the subject of much speculation. Astrologers have noted that at sunrise December 12, 2012, the sun will conjunct the intersection of the Milky Way and the plane of the elliptic creating a cosmic cross. However, traditional Maya scholars believe that convergence of this alignment and this date ending the long count cycle is merely a coincidence. They maintain that ancient Maya astronomers could not have known about the procession of the equinoxes or how we relate to the galactic center.[6]

It has also been postulated that this Long Count date represents a Maya belief that December 21, 2012 will mark the end of time. Mainstream archeologists, however, are not expecting any such event, only another beginning of another cycle, no more exciting than an odometer clicking over. This view is supported by the fact that the Maya calendar continues on beyond 2012 into further units of time beyond *baktun* cycles in factors of 20

TRAUMA: TIME, SPACE and FRACTALS

to *pictun* cycles of 7,900 years, followed by the *calabtun* lasting 158,000 years, then the *kinchiltun* of 3.2 million years, *alatun* 63.1 million years and *hablatun* 1.26 billion years.

While this fugue-like chrono-vision of the long count faded along with collapse of Classic Maya civilization, their non-linear sacred and civil Calendar Round remained in use in many parts of Central and South America until the arrival of the Conquistadors. These inevitably Eurocentric, mercenary newcomers had zero interest in the arcane dimensions of these harmonic calibrations. Who amongst these fortune seekers was qualified to even begin to understand or appreciate the value of an indigenous a calendar system which was able to calculate biologic and environmental cycles, along with multiple levels of other cosmic realties? In keeping with the all-pervasive colonial mentality of their era, they remained willfully blind to any time keeping system whose extensions included a meaningful interconnection with off-world planetary and other cycles, which extended even further into realms far beyond our earthly plane.[7]

With strong armed support from the Spanish Inquisition, and a policy of relentless subjugation, the invaders eventually succeeded in imposing a new order limiting measurement of time to their relatively sterile, Earth-bound, linear, Catholic and commercial calendar. Within the blind loyal faith of this imperial mindset, anything Europeans did not understand, control or dominate was deemed a threat. Nevertheless, the indigenous cultures, not in agreement with this and other attempts to re-order their reality, bravely resisted. As a consequence, countless millions disappeared and died during the violent establishment of this new Colonial Era. The few remaining Time Keepers retreated into obscurity in hopes of keeping at least some of their traditions intact.

Many centuries passed before, long abandoned and deeply hidden, Maya cities were rediscovered by the nineteenth century American adventurer John

TRAUMA: TIME, SPACE and FRACTALS

Lloyd Stephens, "the father of American archeology", and his English travelling companion, the artist and illustrator Frederick Catherwood. These intrepid explorers methodically bushwhacked a seeker's path through stifling heat, humidity, and countless mosquito infested tangles of tropical undergrowth with no guarantee of success. These trials were eventually rewarded by their discovery of forty-four spectacular, time battered ancient sites, each displaying a wonderland of temple complexes replete with a tantalizing wealth of mysterious inscriptions. Their published findings, *Incidents of Travel in Central America, Chiapas and Yucatan* (1841), illustrated with beautifully detailed drawings of vine covered ruins, set off a storm of fascination about the true nature of this extraordinary "lost civilization". Given both class and cultural blind spots inherent within their Victorian era intellectual straightjackets, neither of the two men could conceive of any possibility that "natives", as they called them, who lived in surrounding jungles, could have had anything to do with the history of these ancient artistic and architectural marvels.[8]

Edgar Alan Poe referred to the Stephens and Catherwood accounts as... "Perhaps the most interesting book of travel ever published". In the absence of any documentation, imaginative speculation about these mysterious ruins began with stories of pyramids and cities built by Egyptian and other survivors from the sunken continent of Atlantis. Multiple theories continued to abound involving Lost Tribes of Israel, Asian travelers from Lemuria and Mu and unknown antediluvian beings lost in the night of time.[9] While these somewhat romantic theories were subsequently discredited by late 20th and early 21st century archeologists, a flavor of these speculations has resurfaced in various New Age and alternative archeological interpretations, which now include "intergalactic sky gods" and other extra-terrestrial interventions. However, in view of the most recent terrestrial and underwater excavations revealing compelling evidence of ancient cultures and artifacts for which we have known record, I have come to believe that one cannot totally dismiss the possibility that there did in fact, exist an advanced global civilization with architectural and other remnants scattered throughout the vast territories of our planet.

Here in the Americas, with input from our Asian and European colleagues, twentieth century archeological explorations and excavations eventually transformed a study of Pre-Colombian ruins into a respected, if somewhat esoteric discipline. While some pioneers in the field of Maya studies initially believed that they were a culture of peaceful stargazers, further excavations revealed something quite different. Archeological evidence now presents a picture of a war-like, blood drenched culture obsessed with a complex chrono-cosmology which can now be understood as a profound understanding of non-linear fractal time. Scholarly progress accelerated rapidly during the

TRAUMA: TIME, SPACE and FRACTALS

1960's and 70's as investigators were able to decipher many of the complexities inherent within hieroglyphic writing. This explosion of knowledge continues as new sites are still being uncovered which reveal additional insights into the Maya and other Pre-Columbian histories and cosmologies.

And then quite suddenly, or so it seemed, toward the end of the nineteen eighties, amidst an ethical wasteland of rampant denial, deceit and deception, covert wars and unregulated greed, mysteries of ancient Maya and their cyclical view of ages and stages, re-emerged into popular imagination. In retrospect, this is not so surprising given a credible perception that their social traumas and ongoing challenges mirror those of our own. Along with the Maya and other lost and failed civilizations, we share the realities of perpetual war, drought, disease, famine, trade imbalances, over population, food production and other problems relating to legitimate transfer of political power.

TRAUMA: TIME, SPACE and FRACTALS

Inspired by Native American "Breed", as he describes himself, Tony Shearer, poet and author of *Lord of the Dawn: Return of Quetzalcoatl* (1971), Jose Arguelles Ph.D., (Mexican-American visionary artist, art historian, educator, originator of The Foundation for the Law of Time, and co-founder of Earth Day), published *The Mayan Factor: Path Beyond Technology*. Soon after, he provided the driving force for a planet wide Harmonic Convergence; a global meditation which took place on August 16-17, 1987. These dates were purported to correspond with an auspicious New Age astrological alignment of planets conducive to the arrival of a great shift in Earth's energy, away from warlike conflict towards peaceful coexistence. This idea soon caught on with both mainstream and alternative media sources which recognized a potential for a series of good story events.

According to anthropologist Richard Grossinger, Arguelles' timing dates represent "a somewhat apocryphal date that he pulled out of his rendition of Maya hermeneutics". Tony Shearer had originally believed this to be a time of transition from the Mesoamerican Fifth World to a New Age Sixth World or Sixth Sun. This reasoning is based upon Arguelles' interpretation of a calendar formula derived from a Maya belief in specific events to follow a time of "Thirteen Heavens and Nine Hells", which will serve as a temporal marker announcing a time of transition.[10]

As I understand it, his Harmonic Convergence was organized in a hope that if sufficient numbers gathered to meditate at planetary power centers such as Mt. Shasta, California, Mt. Fuji, Japan, Crestone, Colorado, and Stonehenge, this event could usher in an era of peace and a twenty-five year countdown to the end of the Maya Long Count in 2012. After attending an Arguelles presentation in the San Francisco Bay Area, my husband and I decided to wake our children early and all join the world wide, pre-dawn meditations outdoors in the sheltered privacy of a Redwood grove just above our

TRAUMA: TIME, SPACE and FRACTALS

North Berkeley garden. At that time we had three cats, an orange Main Coon, two Siamese Chocolate Points, as well as a cantankerous Lady Chow, all of whom remained in some state of permanent contention. On this morning however, they followed along quietly, as we lit a few small candles and waited for sunrise over San Francisco Bay.

As I recall, the energy of that morning was in fact, extraordinarily peaceful, even amongst our extremely territorial animal friends. For a brief moment, I experienced a clear vision of our entire planet covered in an intricate network of light. Later, I came to believe that this image that I "envisioned" was probably a template of the internet that was preparing to manifest a new option for global connection and communication. Soon however, our early morning harmonics gradually faded away into more mundane concerns.

Shortly thereafter, it became increasingly clear that whatever time it was, did not have much to do with harmonics within my immediate family or the larger world situation or so it seemed at the time. In retrospect, I believe that it would be interesting to re-examine the possibility that the Harmonic Convergence was in fact a significant temporal marker. That and the surrounding era has emerged as a time of significant convergences that combined to shift our understanding of both consciousness and time itself. Along with an interest in Mayan culture and civilization, Native American spirituality and Hindu cosmology, Mandelbrot's discovery of fractal geometry also emerged at this time of psychedelic exploration. Some of these explorations gave rise to Terrence McKenna's research with time waves, the I Ching, and his rediscovery of the fact that both time and human DNA are fractal phenomena.

TRAUMA: TIME, SPACE and FRACTALS

2

CHECKING THE TIME

Soon after the widespread coverage of the Harmonic Convergence, media interest quickly faded and moved on. Apprehensions were now growing about the approach of Y2K, also known as "the year 2000 problem" or "millennium bug". There were fears that older computer hardware and software would be unable to recognize the century change in date resulting in massive data processing chaos. While this turned out to be a non-event, the media continued their focus upon the inevitable, often bizarre and increasingly dire predictions of soothsayers and fundamentalist religions, around the arrival of a new millennium. For some, looking beyond the Bible and our linear Gregorian calendar to ascertain the spiritual nature of admittedly difficult times, ongoing cycles of the Hindu calendar seemed to provide some answers. Over time, Hindu cosmology has gradually made its way into the Western imagination. This process was helped along with well-publicized trips to India made by the Beatles and other glitterati. Alternative media began to popularize Guru Maharishi, and other Eastern teachers who began travelling to the West in order to share their distinctly different view of time and space and karma. This was also a time when psychedelic substances arrived upon the global media scene. These potent cultural de-conditioning, pharmacological and botanical agents opened new doors of perception, a widespread questioning of our status quo and access to realms outside of linear time.

Among the most visible of the New Age spiritual teachers, Baba Ram Dass, formerly known as Harvard psychologist Dr. Richard Alpert, succeeded in popularizing the use of psychedelics along with some of the basic tenets of Hindu philosophy. His paperback edition of *Be Here Now* quickly became a spiritual classic and he has remained a popular figure on the international media circuit. Expecting that his appearance on the U.C. Berkeley campus would draw a large crowd, my family arrived early and waited patiently in line outside along with hundreds of others. Upon entry, we were surprised to find Ram Dass himself, quietly standing just inside the doors, patiently greeting each arrival. At some point, it became clear to campus fire marshals that this very large lecture hall would soon fill to capacity. People would have to be turned away. Local authorities informed our speaker of this need to close doors and that, for safety reasons, those remaining outside would not be permitted to enter. Clearly living in a more spacious reality beyond the obvious, Ram Dass was not concerned…. "Who knows," he offered, "they might be the lucky ones". In subsequent years, Ram Dass has often recounted this ancient tale of "Who Knows", which he shared with us that evening.

The story goes something like this: There was a farmer whose only horse ran away. Friends and neighbors came by to commiserate with his loss saying "this so difficult, so unfair". All the farmer said was "who knows". Eventually, his horse returned and brought along a mate and soon the farmer had many horses. Friends and neighbors then rejoiced at his good fortune. All the farmer said was "who knows". And then, when the farmer's son fell from one of these horses and broke his leg, again there were condolences for this misfortune. And again he said only "who knows". Soon thereafter soldiers came to the farm to look for young men to conscript for the army's ongoing wars. They didn't take his boy with a broken leg... "How fortunate" people said, and the farmer again replied... "who knows"...

This very different and also clear take on reality was a breath of fresh air to my decidedly uptight, graduate student, left brain, linear thinking sensibilities. Yes, it's true that things are not always as they seem, and one should be careful about jumping to conclusions. Yet, this marvelous folk story also resonates not only with "relative reality" but also takes on the perceptual dynamics of quantum physics. This became apparent in Werner Heisenberg's iconic experiments demonstrating that light can be both a particle and a wave and that outcomes are influenced by the consciousness of the observer. In other words, reality is interactive, subject to change and there is no such thing as pure objectivity.

During the course of Ram Dass' presentation an earnest young student stood up to share that this invitation to "be here now" and to be "present in present time", was not appealing to anyone who could look around and see increasingly terrible things happening throughout our modern world. "You need to know what time it is" our speaker replied, "this is the *Kali Yuga*, a time of darkness and despair. All you can do is look around your own life and be of service wherever and whenever you can". While most Hindu scholars may agree that the *Kali Yuga* began around 3102 BC, according to Gregorian calculations, many believe that this era will last 432,000 years and there is not much agreement as to when it will end.

In Hindu scriptures, the *Kali Yuga* is the last in an ongoing cycle of four ages or *Yugas* that our world moves through as part of a larger cycle that began with the *Satya Yuga*, a Golden Age of light, peace, wisdom, and enlightenment. This was followed by the *Treta Yuga*, a Silver Age of virtue and decrease in enlightenment. The third cycle or *Dvapara Yuga* or Bronze Age is an era when human character is divided between virtue and sin, with further decline in enlightenment, self- reflection and awareness. Some of the aspects of this next fourth and most difficult era of greatest darkness for mankind appear in a discourse from the *Mahabharata*, a Sanskrit epic circ 400 BCE.

The *Kali Yuga* or Iron Age is described as an era of ongoing individual and social trauma. This is a time when unreasonable rulers levy unfair taxes and no longer honor their responsibility to promote spirituality. These dishonorable rulers will present an ongoing danger to the world.

Famine and death will be common. Desperate, starving, panic driven populations will begin to migrate toward any territory offering ample grains, edible food and potable water sources. In the realm of relationships, during the *Kali Yuga*, avarice, wrath and animosity will be the new norm. People will harbor cruel and murderous thoughts, without guilt and the helpless will become targets to be preyed upon. Lust will become socially acceptable, sex considered to be a central necessity, while virtue will fade and then cease altogether. Any and all vows of trust will soon be broken and there will be rampant addiction to toxic and intoxicating substances. People will be overwhelmed from work and seek solace in escape and retreat. Wisdom keepers will not be respected. Followers will distort and reject the teachings of their leaders and attempt to cause them harm.[11] One might agree that this dark view of a past, present and future humanity, doomed to suffer the above tribulations and more, seems uncomfortably familiar, especially to those of us who follow current events and also study history as well as individual, social and global trauma. However, the *Kali Yuga* end dates are vague at best and most estimates are located in a future beyond present lifetimes.

Then, a new element in the search for the nature of time, space and reality appeared from the field of mathematics, through the work of Benoit Mandelbrot (1924-2010). While he had published his findings a decade earlier, it was not until the re-issue of *The Fractal Geometry of Nature* in 1982 that his vision received widespread recognition. Now known as the Father of Fractal Geometry, Mandelbrot coined the word "fractal" from the Latin root *fractus* suggesting fragmentation, broken and discontinuous. Unlike the smooth linear shapes of Euclidian geometry, this new geometry of irregular shapes revealed a mathematical order intrinsic to the seeming disorder found in Nature. Mandelbrot argued that seemingly random natural shapes are actually composed of a single, self-similar, repeating pattern observable at any scale. In a cauliflower, for example, a cut through any of the florets reveals the same design throughout the whole cauliflower, at a smaller scale. Each part is like the whole, only smaller.

Hidden in plain sight, the discovery of fractal geometry revealed a mathematical order within an apparent randomness and disorder of the natural world. One finds the pattern of the Fibonacci spiral, for example, manifest in the shell of a chambered nautilus, spiral galaxies, weather systems, whirlpools and fiddlehead ferns. One of the most familiar examples is a branching pattern found in trees, river deltas, lightning streaks, blood vessels, lines in our hands and feet and the dendrites found throughout the human nervous system. One can readily observe these fractal patterns by just pressing gently on closed eyelids in well lit surroundings. Sometimes called, "the fingerprints of God", fractals reveal the inter-connectedness of all Nature. This discovery also holds important implications for our understanding of the uneven fabric of time.[12]

The notion of fractal time was taken up by Terrence McKenna, (1946-2000) ethno-botanist, psychonaut, performance artist and self–described anarchist, whose extraordinary career navigated a wide range of territory between science and shamanism. After ingesting vast quantities of the *stropharia cubensis* mushroom, which carried him far beyond the restraints of Newtonian physics, he experienced a revelatory conception of the nature of time. In *True Hallucinations* he describes his changing perception:

Quite unexpectedly, what I now propose…is a revision of the mathematical description of time used in physics…According to this theory, the old notion of time as pure duration, visualized as a smooth plane or straight line, is to be replaced by the idea that time is a very complex fractal phenomena with many ups and downs of many sizes over which the probabilistic universe of becoming must flow like water over a boulder strewn riverbed.[13]

Now as we find ourselves at the dawn of the twenty first century, world renowned scientists are telling us that the Universe and time itself consists of cycles unfolding within cycles *ad infintum.* According to Professors Roger Penrose and Vahe Gurzadyan, the Universe did not begin with a linear progression in the wake of the Big Bang some 13.7 billion years ago. Contrary to the previous inflationary, expanding and evolutionary model, they maintain that the Universe is composed of an infinite succession of expanding and collapsing aeons. Here we have a cosmology which includes a vision of non-linear time that resonates with the essence of McKenna's revelation. This seemingly new theory also recalls the ancient wisdom of the Hindu scriptures, which hold that the Universe is periodically destroyed, created and reborn over the vast period of time described in the *yuga* cycles. Penrose and Gurzadyan's modern cosmology also resonates with the fugue-like chrono-vision of the Maya calendars and their interlocking almanacs, wherein each part is a reflection of the whole, in other words, fractal.[14]

In *Fractal Time,* geologist Greg Braden suggests that within this very definition of a fractal, as a pattern that repeats itself in self similar ways on different scales, may also lie a description of a special relationship between us and time. Braden speculates that here, within the mysteries of deep time and the cosmos, one can find resonance throughout the patterns of history in our community systems as well as our individual and family lives. The message in the ancient axiom "As above, so below; as below, so above", sets forth the resonance between microcosm and macrocosm.[15] While this may seem too esoteric a stretch for those of us who work with trauma, the fact remains that the shock of overwhelming life events profoundly affects the way the individual nervous system experiences time. This is also true for social trauma, whereby groups, tribes, communities and even entire nations can also become disoriented in both time and space. Eventually, I came to understand that underlying the seeming chaos of traumatic events, involving both single persons and groups, one could often discern self-similar, repetitive, patterns. It was becoming increasingly evident that these patterns, that one can observe moving within individual and family lives, also manifest through the many layers of larger social systems.

This phenomenon first came to my attention in 1997 during one of many conversations with Bert Hellinger, principle founder of Systemic Constellation Work. I was invited to participate in one of his pilot programs, because he was interested in knowing more about trauma. At that time he was especially interested in social trauma and I was fascinated with his ability to navigate the Informational Field. We were in the UK for a constellation intensive carried out in three British prisons. At that time, Hellinger wanted to work with murderers and other violent offenders in order to gain a deeper understanding of the perpetrator/victim dynamic. As we worked together with these prisoners, who kindly volunteered to share their stories, it became increasingly clear that many were also victims within ongoing patterns of violence. It also became clear that these patterns involved both victims and perpetrators that extended back through many generations. In constellation after constellation we began to discern something like self-similar, non-linear fractal patterns moving through a single lifetime as well as through families, clans, tribes and other social systems.

After our daily work in the prisons, we had an opportunity to visit with our teacher in a more relaxed atmosphere over dinner. As a newcomer and the only American in our small group involved in this endeavor, I was feeling both shy and irrepressibly curious. At the first opportunity, I ventured my observation that he was in fact working with both social trauma and fractals. "Yes", he said, "but I had not seen it exactly that way". Hellinger then explained that his vision was somewhat like a Kirlinian photograph. In these photos, it has been shown that after a part of a leaf is torn away after the first photograph, a faint glow or coronal image of the missing piece appears in the second photograp, showing the original wholeness. In other words, when Bert Hellinger sits together with a client, he begins to see something like a delicate fragment of a vein in a leaf, next the entire leaf, stem, branch, tree and then the whole forest....and beyond. I then realized that it was time to re-think absolutely everything that I thought I knew about the dynamics of family systems, as well as individual, social and even global trauma.

Bert Hellinger returned to this subject of fractals in a conversation with Gabriele ten Hovel in

TRAUMA: TIME, SPACE and FRACTALS

Acknowledging What Is (1999). In a chapter entitled *Space,* he says:

Perhaps the concept of fractals can illustrate what happens. Nobel Prize winner Gerd Binnig, in his book, *Aus Dem Nichts* (Out of Nothing) postulates the thesis that before the evolution of material and spirit, there must have been an evolution of space. Space arranges itself symmetrically and the arrangements repeat themselves. A leaf is constructed like the tree – every leaf is different, but each follows the same order.

When I set up a family, the individuals who are standing there can feel what's going on in this family even though the real family members may be far away. The orders within the family repeat themselves in the constellation. Through a constellation I suddenly have access to a reality that is not accessible to me through the thought process. Something comes to light which has previously been invisible. When it is out in the open, I can look to see if there is a resolution there.

But in the same way that the real family is present in the constellation, the resolution of the representative family also has an effect, in return, on the real family. Something returns to the system, even if they don't know anything about it.

TRAUMA: TIME, SPACE and FRACTALS

Ten Hovel: "Because there is a connection in space"?

Hellinger: "I can't explain it".[16]

Hellinger then recounts a situation in which there was a young woman who had made an unsuccessful suicide attempt. Setting up a constellation revealed that it was actually her mother who was suicidal. And then it emerged that the mother's father had drowned himself, so now there were three generations involved in this pattern. The girl attempted suicide in place of her mother, out of blind love and loyalty, and her mother wanted to follow her own father into death. A representative for the grandfather was then introduced into the constellation and placed next to the girl's mother. The resolution was for the mother to lean against her own father and for the daughter to say "I am staying".

This constellation was taking place on a Sunday morning in Switzerland and the girl's mother was at home in Germany. While the constellation was taking place, the girl's mother was out walking her dog. Her usual path crossed over the bridge where her father had drowned himself. Every time she crossed that bridge she would stand at the railing looking upstream to the place where her father had died and say a prayer for him. On this particular morning, as she crossed the bridge and was about to say her prayer, she felt an impulse guide her to the opposite side of the bridge. On that other side she felt a happiness that she couldn't explain. As she now looked downstream, she suddenly felt that she could swim with the currents of life. All thoughts of suicide disappeared along with this experience. Something had generated a healing effect over a spatial distance without that woman knowing anything about what was happening in the family constellation.[17]

Those with experience in systemic constellation work know that stories such as these are quite familiar. For me, however, all of this was something quite new. And there was much that I did not yet understand. Nevertheless, one thing was very clear and that was that upon a return to the USA my work was going to evolve from an individual to a systemic perspective.

Over time, I have come to appreciate the importance of navigating both linear and non-linear time in understanding and resolving trauma as well as seeing each individual as an integral part of a series of larger inter-connected systems. From this perspective, when one is working with one person, one needs to bear in mind the possible repercussions of any intervention upon the systems within which this person is also a part. In this holistic and systemic view, it becomes increasingly clear that in engaging each seemingly isolated overwhelming event that presents itself as trauma, we often find ourselves also delving into the realms of today's most pressing and intractable global issues.

TRAUMA: TIME, SPACE and FRACTALS

3

THE REPLICATING FRACTAL OF KATYN

April is the cruelest month, breeding
Lilacs out of the dead land, mixing,
Memory and desire, stirring
Dull roots with spring rain.
Winter kept us warm, covering
Earth in forgetful snow....

(T.S. Eliot, The Burial of the Dead)

As far as I know, there have not been many serious studies devoted to *unresolved* social traumas which tend to replicate throughout family and social systems. In general, however, it has been observed that many replicating traumas tend to occur on the anniversary of previous traumas, especially those involving broken connections and various forms of loss. While internationally known clinicians including Anne Ancelin Shutzenberger, Bert Hellinger, Peter Levine and Monica McGoldrick, have observed this phenomena, it has often been seen only as a novelty and not yet recognized as a topic worthy of serious study within the field of social traumatology. While I can accept the reality of coincidence as a possible factor in replicating traumas, in the case of politically motivated events such as the Oklahoma Bombing, and Columbine High School Massacre, we know that their April 19th and 20th dates were deliberately chosen as anniversaries of previous traumatic events. This is also the case around many events surrounding the now iconic date of 9/11 including the Palestinian terrorist group Black September's, September 11th killing of 11 Israeli hostages at Munich Olympic Games where date, place and number of victims were part of the message. In *A Question of Balance* I explored these April and September dates in some depth along with biologist Rupert Sheldrake's notion that places also have "fields of memory" that can also play a role in traumatic repetitions. One of these places is a dark forest surrounding the Russian village of Katyn.

TRAUMA: TIME, SPACE and FRACTALS

On April 10, 2010 a plane carrying the Polish president and his delegation en route to Russia to commemorate the 70th anniversary of a massacre of Polish leadership in the Katyn forest in Smolensk, crashed in this same forest at Smolensk. All aboard were killed, including many descendants of victims of the Katyn forest massacre of April 1940. Not surprisingly, the shock of this recent tragedy evoked a sinister resonance with the event that this journey was meant to both acknowledge and remember and opened a new wound over an old scar. Replicating traumas such as this prompts a return to questions of connections, co-incidence, consequences and the presence of a larger pattern within collective experience. [18]

Both national tragedies around Katyn, of April 1940 and April 2010 are now taking their place in the wider context of past Polish-Russian relations. Each persists in mutually negative stereotypes and one finds more continuity than change in their long entangled histories. Russia has played a dominant role in Polish political life, in one way or another since the early 1700s, when Russian Tsars first began to dominate Polish politics. Catherine the Great annexed most of Poland and these fertile agricultural lands were ruled by Russia until 1915 when German and Austro-Hungarian armies pushed them out. Nevertheless, most Russians persisted in the belief that Polish territory was their domain, while most Poles resisted. During the World War II era, Polish people suffered both as victims and perpetrators but most see themselves only as victims. In modern times, during and after their occupation by the former USSR, most Poles view Russia as the foremost enemy of Polish independence. Most Russians, in turn, view the Poles as an ongoing threat to the security of their border. [19]

As a result, we have large scale social trauma where whole groups are in need of some movement toward mutual completion so that the grievances can be released into the past. As long as there is no resolution, whole nations remain in a field of trauma which is carried into subsequent generations. This sets the stage for traumatic re-enactment and the madness of re-creating old traumas which serve only to perpetuate the pain.

Katyn, and a series of events which came to be known as the Katyn Forest Massacre, first came to my attention in an award winning film by Andrzej Wajda which appeared in 2007 just before my first trip to Poland. I had been invited by a German colleague who was working with groups in Western Poland in a formerly German area where she had family roots before the Soviets moved the border and expelled ethnic Germans. While having had some experience working with war trauma in both Germany and Russia, I had never been to Poland, which has long suffered the historical misfortune of being located between these historically adversarial regimes determined to crush their sovereignty. In August 1939, Pre-war Poland was divided between the Third Reich and the Soviet Union according to the terms of the Ribbentrop-Molotov Pact. The nightmare of this reality is evoked in the opening scene of Wajda's *Katyn* which takes place on a bridge in September of 1939. Swarms of desperate people appear in a process of fleeing in opposite directions, carrying whomever and whatever they could manage. German forces were advancing from the West while the Red Army was rapidly invading from the East.

At that time, Polish law required all university graduates to serve as officers in their reserve army. As the Russian occupation took hold, Stalin and his Politburo ordered victorious troops to round up these reservists and other military personnel and deport them as Polish prisoners of war to Russia. In the film, these events are related through the eyes of women; mothers, wives, sisters and daughters of these captured deportees. For years, many wondered and waited for the return of their fathers, husbands, brothers and sons. Stalin maintained that they had all escaped to Manchuria. We now know that circumstances surrounding their disappearance were quite different. In April of 1940, the dictator and his Politburo had issued another order to Soviet NKVD agents (secret police and predecessors of the KGB) in Poland. They were to carry out the "liquidation" of the entire Polish elite, including Mr. Wajda's father.

During these brutal machine-like operations, one by one, each prisoner was killed with bayonets and a pistol shot to the back of the head. Those that resisted, and there were many, had choke knots tied around their necks. The victim's hands were tied to the choke knots and pulled sharply up toward their shoulder blades. If they continued to struggle, they were simply strangled to death. Murdered Poles were then shoveled into several huge pits including those in a forest surrounding the village of Katyn in the Russian region of Smolensk. This small wooded area, located along the banks of the River Dieppe became a gravesite for many of the 21,857 murdered Poles and a festering wound in Polish and Russian relations. As Wajda's film makes clear, the intent of this atrocity was not only to destroy Poland's military capability but also to purge her educated population of engineers, civil servants, clergy, intellectuals, physicians and any other citizen whose expertise could enable their country to function independently. [20]

As the war continued, advancing German forces arrived in Smolensk during spring of 1943. As their forest floors began to thaw, locals saw wolves digging for bones and tipped off the Germans. Troops soon discovered mass burials and carefully began to exhume thousands of corpses. On April 13,1943, Propaganda Minister Joseph Goebbels seized this unexpected opportunity to promote Nazism as a protector against Bolshevik terror. Soon thereafter, the winds of war shifted, and then Stalin took his turn, and blamed the Nazis for this atrocity. Later in April, Polish Prime Minister in Exile, General Wladyslaw Sikorski became extremely skeptical of Stalin's version of the Katyn forest findings, charged Stalin with war crimes and demanded that the International Red Cross investigate. On April 25, 1943 Stalin retaliated by breaking off diplomatic relations with Sikorski's government-in-exile. Very shortly thereafter, the Polish General died in a *mysterious plane crash, attributed to pilot error and mechanical failure.* Stalin's falsified version of Katyn was readily embraced in the court of international opinion and further enforced by the usual police state means. Although fully informed and aware of the truth, Britain, France and the USA chose to turn a blind eye for fear of risking the ire of their Russian allies.[21]

This obfuscation of one of the signature crimes of Stalinism remained unchallenged until April 13, 1990 when Soviet authorities finally admitted responsibility for a massacre of thousands of Poles in the Katyn forest, Smolensk and elsewhere.

TRAUMA: TIME, SPACE and FRACTALS

Exactly, 47 years after Goebbles' announcement, Soviet admission of guilt came in a statement from their Tass news agency under the personal authority of Premier Mikhail Gorbachev. This admission, however, was modified by a serious and also transparent effort to reduce the number of prisoners killed and missing. Nevertheless, the Polish government responded positively with a statement declaring that the question of responsibility for this massacre had "weighed particularly painfully" on Polish-Soviet relations and that a "long awaited" Soviet admission made possible a relationship based on "partnership and true friendship". This official Polish statement goes on to assert that "reconciliation can only be built on truth", even though the whole truth about the total number and location of their dead and missing was not yet, and may never be, known. [22]

With the election of devout Catholic, ultra-conservative Lech Kaczynski to the Polish presidency in 2005, it was clear that reconciliation with Russia was not going to be easy. Although the Polish people suffered as victims and perpetrators, and some controversial combination of both during the events of the Second World War; for Mr. Kaczynski, victim consciousness remained uppermost. As a fierce nationalist, this new president was a dogged critic of Vladimir Putin and Russia's efforts to restore influence over Poland and other areas of their former Soviet Union. He accused Russia of blackmail, manipulation and suggested EU sanctions against them for economic bullying. Kaczynski vigorously supported the Republic of Georgia throughout its conflicts with Russia, and vetoed talks on co-operation between the EU and Russia. Furthermore, he hoped to free Europe from dependence on Russian gas by increasing Poland's own production of gas extracted from shale. This proposal would have made his country the largest supplier of this type of fuel. Tensions increased when Kaczynski accepted a US proposal to build a nuclear missile shield along Poland's eastern border facing Russia.[23]

Nevertheless, Lech Kaczynski had made it clear that, as President, one key initiative of his career was to achieve greater openness and recognition from Russia about the Katyn Forest Massacre of Polish prisoners by Soviet Secret Police. He remained adamant that their two countries could not normalize relations until they achieved some degree of reconciliation around these crimes. Then in April 2010, Prime Minister Vladimir Putin, in an unprecedented gesture of apparent good will, offered to commemorate these mass executions alongside of a Polish leader. The response of the Polish government was divided. While President Kaczynski stood firm in his claim to higher moral ground of victimization only, the more accommodating Prime Minister Donald Tusk was invited to fly to Smolensk for an April 7th day of commemoration to stand together with Mr. Putin in Katyn.

During this ceremony of acknowledgment, Mr. Putin refused to cede any high moral ground to

Poland or that Katyn was a war crime. According to his version of events, Stalin ordered this massacre of Polish prisoners as revenge for the 1920 deaths of 32,000 Red Army soldiers in Polish prisoner of war camps, who had died of starvation and disease. Furthermore, he maintained that *in 1940 Poland did not exist as an independent state,* and therefore *the Polish prisoners were, in fact, Soviet citizens* who had shared the fate of millions of *other Soviet citizens.* (It is now known that Stalin dwarfed Hitler's crimes by murdering 30 million of his own people). Mr. Putin's address emphasized the fact that under Stalin, whole social classes became victims; professors, clergymen, peasants, cossacks, and former officers from the Tsarist army were not spared. According to this version, with both Poles and Russians now in roles of both perpetrators and victims, one could imagine that some possibility for genuine re-conciliation may have briefly existed. However, this version of Poles as Soviet citizens, sharing martyrdom with other Russian Soviet citizens, was not acceptable to the Polish president.

TRAUMA: TIME, SPACE and FRACTALS

Soon thereafter, and despite the fact that he was not invited, Lech Kaczynski announced his plans to fly from Warsaw and arrive in Katyn on Saturday April 10th along with a delegation of 80 officials and relatives of the victims of the massacre. "I hope that I get a visa", he joked while announcing his plans to deliver an address, very different than that of Mr. Putin. In his own address, President Kaczynski intended to make clear that Polish prisoners were *"citizens of the Second Republic of Poland, people who formed the foundation of our statehood, who adamantly served the Motherland..."* [24]

Then in a chilling twist, just as Russia and Poland were attempting to come to terms with Katyn, a large portion of the country's leadership was once again demolished, together with many descendants of the first Katyn tragedy. According to multiple news reports, the President's Soviet Era Tupolev-154, recently renovated and repaired in Russia, crashed near Katyn forest in Smolensk. It was reported that the President, his wife, head of the national bank, chairman of the Olympic committee, *all senior military officers*, other officials, dignitaries and relatives of Katyn victims were on board. All 96 passengers and crew had died. The tragic irony of this disaster was not lost on Russian officials who expressed their shock and grief, "The soul can only shudder from the realization that Katyn has claimed more victims", said Konstantin Kosachyov, head of the foreign affairs committee of Russia's parliament. Prime Minister Putin immediately took personal charge of the crash investigation and all forensics were carried out in Russia. After an allegedly thorough investigation, Russia announced that the entire blame for this catastrophe rests with Poland due to inexperienced pilot error, language problems, unruly passengers and heavy fog.

This explanation was readily accepted by most of our corporate controlled mainstream media, some of which also warned of conspiracy theorists who could complicate the necessary grieving processes.

Nevertheless, serious doubts and alternate versions of this "tragic co-incidence" quickly surfaced. It was soon revealed that Arkadiusz Prostasiuk, the Polish air force pilot of the presidential plane was very experienced, had flown this route many times and was fluent in Russian. Eye witnesses reported minimal fog at the landing site at the time of the crash. No one seems to be able to explain why so many key government officials were allowed to travel on the same aircraft or why there were no journalists on board. Vladimir Putin's former advisor, Andrei Illarionov, signed an open letter written by Russian dissidents voicing concern about the conduct of this investigation. According to this letter, "rapprochement with the current Russian authorities is more important for this Polish government than determining the truth about this plane crash in Smolensk". [25]

As might be expected, independent and alternative media coverage on less controlled internet sources introduced further doubts. Long standing Polish distrust of anything Russian was further fueled by the appearance of a shaky hand-held cell phone video, purportedly of the smoldering presidential plane crash, posted on international You Tube channels. This was soon followed by a hastily assembled, Dutch documentary, *Letter from Poland,* casting numerous aspersions upon the official story. As one commentator pointed out, Vladimir Putin has a history of using dates to send messages. The most outspoken critic of his policies, journalist Anna Politkovskya was assassinated on Mr. Putin's birthday. As this documentary reviews the crash site video, *whose authenticity has not been verified,* one sees no evidence of 96 bodies, or any personal belongings, whatsoever, only a few shadowy figures moving around the wooded site. The audio portion is in Russian and one hears cries of "don't shoot us", four pistol shots, and then "let's get out of here". A male voice then cries out in expletives and "you won't get away with this". There are several postings of this video with sub-titles in English and also in Polish. Soon thereafter it was revealed that Andrei Menderey, the Ukrainian man who had shot this video of the crash site, had been stabbed in Kiev on April 15 and taken to the hospital in critical condition. On April 16th, unidentified individuals entered the hospital, unplugged him from life support and stabbed him three more times, thus ensuring silence. Andrei Menderey's brutal death ended any chance of exposing to the public, whatever else he may have seen or heard at and around the Katyn forest crash site. Russian sources deemed this murder to be another co-incidence. [26]

On the scene and amongst throngs of mourners attending the April 18th funeral proceedings in Krakow for the Polish president and his wife Maria, Austrian science and investigative reporter Jane Burgermeister's video coverage added further fuel to the burgeoning conspiracies. Always controversial and never one to bow to pressures of political correctness, she dared to mention details of this crash video and the subsequent assassination of Andrei Menderey in Kiev. Furthermore, she related conversations with Polish citizens, whom she declined to name, who maintained that their president and his delegation were in fact never aboard that plane. There were, she maintains, widespread suspicions that they were kidnapped and executed and their bodies burned beyond recognition. Only a "skeleton crew" was aboard that doomed flight and those few survivors were immediately eliminated at the crash site. If that wasn't enough, she noted that high level delegations from Britain, France, Germany and the USA did not attend the funeral proceedings. While excuses were offered that a volcanic ash cloud prevented travel, she remarked that anyone attending or watching on video can see that skies over Krakow and most of Europe were a very clear blue on that day. Shortly thereafter, Ms. Burgermeister was arrested and detained in Vienna. Several months later she was released without charges, presumably in exchange for her silence, which she has scrupulously maintained since that time. [27]

For Poles, this crash was a great shock at the time and also a collision with their past. As Former President Aleksander Kwasniewski lamented "Katyn is a cursed place. It sends shivers down my spine. The first flower of the Second Polish Republic is murdered in the forests around Smolensk, now the elite of the Third Polish Republic die in this tragic aircraft accident while approaching Smolensk airport". Pro-Russian political opponents of President Kaczynski and his brother are now in charge of the upper echelons of government. [28]

In November 2010, Law and Justice party members Anna Fotyga and Antoni Macierewicz traveled to Washington DC with a petition signed by 300,000 citizens from the Association of Katyn Families (*Stowarzyszenia Rodzin*) calling for the US government to launch an independent international investigation into the April, 10th crash. This petition was accompanied by an open letter from Jaroslaw Kaczynski, former Prime Minister and identical twin of the deceased president, who had himself narrowly survived an assassination attempt one month earlier. As in 1943, the Polish request for help was ignored as *again*, the State Department had no interest in complicating their relationship with the Russians.[29]

From a systemic perspective, we might view this April 2010 plane crash tragedy, as yet another iteration in a long, tortuous fractal of victim and perpetrator dynamics that have characterized Russian-Polish relations for many generations. One is then motivated to ask how these kinds of fractals get started and what is needed to resolve this ongoing pain? As a traumatolgist, my experience has been that patterns repeat in individual lives and family systems when something in need of resolution is denied, interrupted or covered up. In the case of the Katyn tragedies of 1940 and 2010, and other social traumas that have occurred along specific timelines, this has always been the case.

TRAUMA: TIME, SPACE and FRACTALS

These patterns perpetuate, as French psychiatrist, Anne Ancelin Shutzenberger set forth in *The Ancestor Syndrome* when "what must not be forgotten, must also not be remembered". This legacy has had a profound impact upon family dynamics and also the relationship between men and women.

In a recent article in *The Knowing Field*, "Conceptual Constellations: The History of Nations, Cultures and Religions", Joy Manne wrote about her experiences with Systemic Constellation Work in Poland. During a seminar in Warsaw a participant stated that "Men and Women cannot relate in Poland". This was not surprising to Manne who knew that Polish territory has suffered through many wars. At the beginning of her work there she reports feeling as though she was standing knee deep in blood and mud. This field of death weighs heavily on relationships. Manne observes that:

"When a country has been fighting war after war for many generations, every father and husband is already a dead soldier and every boy born is already a soldier who will die. Women must support each other to survive"...... "If women do not see men as alive, they also do not see them as long-term investments with regard to relationships. Therefore they cannot commit themselves to the men and their husbands cannot come first. If boys, young men and husbands experience themselves as already dead in battle they cannot fully invest in life." [30]

During the workshop, Manne "saw an image" and then asked all of the men to move to one side the room and the women to the other. This event took place in a large room with a group of about fifty people. Nearly two thirds of the men then fell to the floor in postures recognized as those of fallen soldiers. The women gathered together in small groups. After a long time, a few of these women looked toward the few men who remained standing. One woman then said that she saw them as dead; all the men were dead. Then the women started to grieve and hold onto each other for support. The still standing men were interested in this and welcomed the women who began to move toward them. Slowly these women began to interact with the men who welcomed them, took their hands, looked into their eyes and some were able to embrace. Manne asked the women to tell the men that they were interacting with: "Now I see that you are alive." More women then crossed the room to go to the men.

Manne reports that after several years of constellation work in Poland done by herself and others, her feeling of being mired in mud and blood has disappeared. She has come to believe that systemic constellation work has the potential to heal not only families but the larger energy fields of countries, as well. [31]

4

JAPAN: LAND OF THE SETTING SUN

*I have become Shiva
Destroyer of Worlds....*

(J. Robert Oppenheimer "Father" of the Atomic Bomb)

*We may not be able to live in Japan someday-
Radiation is going to be flowing out for a long period
of time*

(Ichiro Ozawa, Senior Politician, May, 2011)

Oppenheimer's prophetic words have become something like a mantra for an ongoing nightmare of nuclear destructive capability. Our official story of America as victim and Japan as perpetrator begins on December 7, 1941 with a surprise, unprovoked, Japanese attack on the Pearl Harbor naval installation in Hawaii. I was born in 1943 and this was the version which I learned in school and grew up with. In our conservative post-war community it was considered un-patriotic to question our government's version of wartime community it was considered un-patriotic to question our government's version of wartime activities. Now, however, we live in a very different world. As a result of declassified files released in the Freedom of Information Act, it appears that this attack was neither a surprise nor was it unprovoked. Furthermore, the US was actually complicit in events of this so called "Day of Infamy". With citizens in an isolationist mood, government officials knew that only a direct attack on US territory could justify an entry into World War II. Among this abundance of new information we find the testimony of Lt. Colonel Clifford M. Andrew, former US Army intelligence officer and temporary Assistant Chief of Staff:

Five men were directly responsible for what happened at Pearl Harbor. I am one of those five men...We knew well in advance that the Japanese were going to attack. At least nine months before the Japanese attack on Pearl Harbor I was assigned to prepare for it. I was operating under the direct order of the President of the United States and was ordered not to give vital intelligence information relating to the whereabouts of the Japanese fleet to our commanders in the field. We had broken the Japanese code...we'd been monitoring their communications for months prior to the attack...

For the people of the US both then and now I feel sorrow, for people have been so misled, to have been lied to so much and to have thoroughly believed the lie given to them. [32]

It is often said that "truth is the first casualty of war" and the so called "just" war of World War II was no exception. This new war was a boon to burgeoning military industrial interests and creation of the Manhattan Project. Deeply shrouded in secrecy, this nuclear physics effort under the direction of the US Army Corps of Engineers, with participation from scientists from the UK and Canada, resulted in the development of our first atomic bomb. The first detonation of a nuclear weapon featured a device code named "the gadget" and a trial run was conducted at the Trinity site in

TRAUMA: TIME, SPACE and FRACTALS

New Mexico. This historical event was observed by William L. Laurence, "Atomic Bill", Pulitzer Prize winning science writer for the NY Times who subsequently coined the term "Atomic Age".

This super patriotic journalist and US War Department propaganda master was actually born in an isolated Jewish village in Lithuania that was, in his words, "completely out of space and time"; lacking both electricity and running water. After failed attempts at activism against the Tsar, he arranged to be smuggled across the border from Russia to Germany in a barrel and eventually landed in America. Upon arrival he re-invented himself and changed his name from Leid Sieu to William, for Shakespeare, Leonard for Leonardo Da Vinci and Laurence for the street he came to live on in Massachusetts. His journalistic contributions burned with the zeal of a convert, as he continued to stoke an enthusiastic embrace of his adoptive land and its emerging nuclear narrative. All of his dispatches came to heavily influence the way naïve,

TRAUMA: TIME, SPACE and FRACTALS

God fearing Americans, my family included, came to view their newborn bomb. In his memorable description of the Trinity test explosion, Laurence combined biblical and Genesis-like imagery with religious awe that included worshipful feelings toward the bomb itself. [33]

And just at that instant there rose from the bowels of the earth a light not of this world, the light of many suns in one. It was a sunrise such as the world has never seen, a great green super sun climbing in a fraction of a second to a height of more than eight thousand feet, rising ever higher until it touched the clouds, lighting up the earth and sky all around with a dazzling luminosity.

Up it went, a great ball of fire about a mile in diameter changing colors as it kept shooting upward, from deep purple to orange, expanding, growing bigger, rising as it expanded, an elemental force freed from its bonds after being chained for billions of years. For a fleeting instant the color was unearthly green, such as one sees only in the corona of the sun during a total eclipse. It was as though the earth had opened and the skies had split. One felt as though one were present at the moment of creation when God said "Let there be light". [34]

TRAUMA: TIME, SPACE and FRACTALS

While this journalist's rhetoric is limited here to Judeo-Christian imagery, to my mind, his prose also evokes archetypes of "Prometheus Unchained" and "Bringer of Fire", as well as (fallen) Archangel Lucifer, yet another "Bringer of Light". In fact, Laurence saw science writers as "the true descendants of Prometheus whose task was to 'take the fire from the scientific Olympus; the laboratories and universities, and bring it down to the people. He often invoked such mythological language as part of his Religion of Science. Later, to scientists uncertain of this bomb's efficiency, Laurence wrote:

With the flash came a delayed roll of a mighty thunder head just as the flash was seen for a hundred miles. The roar echoed and reverberated from distant hills... sounding as though it came from some supramundane source, as well as the bowels of the earth. The hills said Yes and the mountains chimed in Yes. It was as if the earth had spoken and the sudden iridescent clouds and sky had joined in one affirmative answer. Atomic energy – Yes. It was like a grand symphony of the elements, fascinating and terrifying, uplifting and crushing, ominous, devastating, full of great promise and great foreboding. [35]

Subsequent and ongoing events have made clear that, by whatever name, the nuclear genii unleashed at Trinity has no intention of *ever* being contained. After the initial euphoria of this explosion subsided, project director Kenneth Bainbridge remarked, "Now, we are all sons of bitches". Weeks later nuclear weapons were unleashed against the people of Japan. Our first bomb dropped on Hiroshima on August 6th, 1945, euphemistically code named "Little Boy", used Uranium-235 as its fission source. Robert Lewis, co-pilot of the *Enola Gay* B29 bomber wrote in his log, "My God, what have we done." Three days later, a second more powerful plutonium fueled bomb, code named "Fat Man" was dropped on Nagasaki. These two thermonuclear devices instantly killed 148,000, mostly civilian men, women and children and many more over time. For survivors there was an immediate terror of extreme heat, missing loved ones, melting flesh, horrific burns, agonizing dehydration, radiation induced vomiting, diarrhea, bleeding from various orifices, hair loss, extreme weakness and often death. By 1950 the death toll was already over 340,000 and growing, as cancer, birth defects, genetic damage, post-traumatic stress and other long term effects took hold. [36]

Days after these bombings, Japan's authoritarian, militaristic government declared an unconditional surrender. Debate continues to rage over the justification of using nuclear weapons against a civilian population. Those who seek to justify this form of mass murder argue that conquest of the Japanese mainland would have cost an estimated 500,000 allied lives. Along with this mind set we have Orwellian justifications that these nuclear weapons "save lives and bring peace". Others maintain that the war in the Pacific was already won after the capture of Okinawa. These disastrous bombings could have been avoided if Japanese peace overtures for a conditional surrender had been accepted in January 1945. Admiral Chester W. Nimitz, Commander of the Pacific Fleet agreed with this view, "The Japanese had, in fact, already sued for peace. The atomic bombs played no decisive part, from a purely military point of view, in the defeat of Japan". [37]

It has been suggested that the bombings were intended to send a message to the Soviets and this event at the end of World War II was also an opening volley in the Cold War with the USSR. With hindsight it appears, to me at least, almost inevitable that our atomic weapons would be detonated, given the vast sums of money they brought to scientists at universities and the self-justifying super structure which became known as the military-industrial complex. And yet, some doubts remained. Over time, the Manhattan Project scientists found that the consequences of atomic warfare were harder to accept in reality than in theory. Frank Oppenheimer, brother of Robert the physicist, expressed the regret of many who developed the atomic bomb. "Somehow we always thought it would not be dropped on people". Even J.R. Oppenheimer himself, the central figure in the development of this weapon was deeply troubled. Reportedly, he turned to then President Harry S. Truman with his feelings of guilt and remorse, "Mr. President, I feel I have blood on my hands." Mr. Truman responded by reaching into his pocket and offering the distressed scientist a neatly folded clean white handkerchief, "Well here, would you like to wipe your hands?"[38] How big a handkerchief, one wonders, would be required to wipe away that much blood?

One of the few voices willing to publically express moral outrage and concern about the looming dangers of radiation, left wing journalist Dwight McDonald decried the dropping of "half-understood poisons" on a civilian populace. Nevertheless, the prevailing mindset was that an innocent, victimized America, humiliated by the Pearl Harbor attack, was entitled to revenge. In a press release of August 6th, 1945 President Truman announced:

The Japanese began the war from the air at Pearl Harbor. They have been repaid many fold. And the end is not yet...It is an atomic bomb. It is harnessing the basic power of the universe. The force from which the sun draws its powers has been loosed against those who brought war to the Far East. [39]

The theme of this statement, invoking military necessity and embrace of nuclear weapons as a near mystical force that confers omnipotence, would reverberate long afterward in official and unofficial rhetoric. As official spokesman for our war department, Laurence flew along on the bombing mission over Nagasaki. This for Laurence was the consummation of his passion for this weapon. His belief in "destiny" allowed him to suppress any compassion for victims "you feel that sense of compassion, and then you say again, 'you had nothing to do with it'. This determination, this destiny, has been decided long ago by forces much greater than any human decision can make or influence". Once more, over Nagasaki he offered a description of the explosion that combined awe, infatuation, and worship of a "living" entity....a new species being born right before our incredulous eyes". [40]

One can only marvel at this paradoxical display of rapture and disconnection. While not specifically using the vocabulary of trauma, or the historical overlay of individual and social trauma, Psychiatrist R.J. Lifton sets forth both psychological and historical themes in Laurence's relationship to nuclear weapons. First, he observes Laurence's personal merger with these weapons, followed by a breakdown of boundaries between man and bomb to an extent that each came to support, enhance and speak for the other. Laurence's merger, over time, also had much to do with his role as official State Department spokesman. He was chosen for that official role precisely because of his passion, scientific knowledge and *apocalyptic imagination.* Laurence placed science at the heart of his own immortality hunger and the world's "destiny". It is not surprising, therefore, that his official, government sanctioned, dispatches to the American people, celebrated a mystical marriage of science and our bomb. Much of this sentiment continues to this day. Senator J. William Fulbright (D. Arkansas) explained this phenomenon as follows:

Power tends to confuse itself with virtue and a great nation is peculiarly susceptible to the idea that its power is a sign of God's favor, conferring upon it a special responsibility for other nations – to make them richer and happier and wiser, to remake them, that is, in its own shining image. [41]

Now in 2011, 66 years after the atomic devastation of Hiroshima and Nagasaki, I struggle to accept that Japan is suffering yet another ongoing nuclear disaster. One wonders how this could happen within a country which has already suffered multiple, acute and chronic dangers posed by radiation. Massive death and mutilation wrought by thermonuclear devices upon the Japanese continues to be transmitted down through the generations. The complexity of this imprint is reflected in the treatment of their *hibakusha,* a Japanese term for the stigma of "those impacted by the explosion". This may be difficult to understand for those of us who are unfamiliar with Japanese culture and belong to systems which have a very different orientation toward victims. Within Japanese reality, exposure to radiation changed the survivor's status as a human being, in his own eyes, as well as others', who now see them as both biologically inferior and dangerous to the unaffected population.

After the bomb, survivors became members of this new group of *hibakusha* and their shame often separated them from the rest of mankind. The marginalizing of *hibakusha* is partly rooted in an ancient Shinto obsession with purification and the fear of contamination. There was also a very real fear of genetic damage within this East Asian culture which stresses family lineage and continuity of generations as a man's central purpose in life in order to symbolically achieve immortality. The marginalization of the *hibakusha* meant discrimination in health care, employment and also marriage negotiations. Survivors were often forced to marry into a lower social class or agree to conditions that would be otherwise unacceptable. [42]

In *Death in Life: Survivors of Hiroshima*, Dr. Lifton explains that one way of dealing with this overwhelming nuclear weapon was to identify with it, or at least, its power. By this means one could hope to share some of the might by which one feels threatened. For many Japanese, a combination of awe and fear sometimes came close to admiration, resembling the psychological defense mechanism of "identification with the aggressor". By this means, one deals with the power one fears by becoming like it, or even part of it.

TRAUMA: TIME, SPACE and FRACTALS

Seeing the bomb as a liberation from Japanese militarism was yet another form of identification. One Japanese scholar, before perishing from its effects, was quoted as saying "The Americans are a great people because anyone who makes such a terrible weapon must have some greatness in them". Nuclear energy was power and the post war Japanese were determined to have it. Overcoming protests by citizens of Hiroshima and Nagasaki, the Japanese nuclear energy program began in 1954. [43] Japan, as geologists, geographers and meteorologists all know, lies directly in the crosshairs of almost every destructive power Mother Nature can unleash. Consider the fact that the Japanese archipelago is located within the so-called Pacific Ring of Fire. This island nation is situated along a junction of four mobile tectonic plates and experiences one fifth of our planet's strongest earthquakes. Therefore, it stands to reason that subsequent construction of 54 nuclear reactors in this precariously unstable earthquake and tsunami zone, crowded with 127 million people, in a nation roughly the size of California, was risky to say the least. Moreover, the Fukushima reactor complex alone, held up to 1,000 times more radiation than the bomb dropped over Hiroshima and is built on reclaimed landfill having a consistency similar to a geological equivalent of tofu. In 2004, one Japanese seismologist warned that the risk of a nuclear accident was "like a kamikaze terrorist wrapped in bombs ready to explode".

Ah, but there was money to be made, lots of it. These reactors were built with political help and heavy investments from British and also American companies; with U.S. Navy designed reactors built by GE and Westinghouse and with work done by Japanese contractors following American protocols. While several nuclear related accidents occurred during the mid-nineties, such as the Tokaimura incident near Tokyo, they were covered up, and safety concerns minimized as a matter of policy. And now in 2011, the course of Japanese history has again been suddenly and violently altered by yet another nuclear nightmare. Their latest catastrophe was of such magnitude that officials couldn't cover it up, and even so, they tried with a vigorous campaign of denial, dis-information, and outright lies. However, in this age of internet and satellite communication, at least some of the truth was out for the world to see; a still unfolding and ongoing global disaster, not yet under control. Nobel laureate Kenzaburo Oe lamented that this latest nuclear accident was like "a third atomic bombing" that Japan inflicted on itself. [44]

The nightmare began on March 11, 2011 on the northeast coast of Japan's main island of Honsu. It was a cool and cloudy Friday afternoon, schools were just letting out, as an undersea quake with a reported magnitude of 9.0 occurred off the Pacific coast of Tohoku. This most powerful seismic event ever known to strike Japan triggered a surge of extremely destructive tsunami waves. Rolling inland with heights comparable to a three story building, a series of waves completely inundated miles of populated coastline. Most people were unable to outrun the wall of advancing waters moving toward them at a speed of 50 miles per hour. Small towns in this region which had dated their history back to the 7th century suddenly ceased to exist. Like the huge cresting wave in Hokusai's iconic woodcut, sea water had easily rolled over shoreline dikes and other defenses. Entire communities disappeared and the mind reels from initial reports estimated 15,698 deaths, 5,715 injured, 4,666 missing across 18 prefectures, as well as over 300,000 refugees suffering shortages of food, water, shelter, medicine and fuel.[45] Along with immediate terrors of shock and loss, individual and collective flashbacks to the massive devastation of Hiroshima and Nagasaki began to emerge in the national psyche. The international media published many stories to this effect and published extensive photos of the bombed cities juxtaposed with recent images of tsunami devastation.[46]

TRAUMA: TIME, SPACE and FRACTALS

Flashbacks to earlier times, places and experiences are to be expected in such a massive field of overwhelm, especially when a previous generation has also been massively traumatized. While Japan engineered a brave and impressive recovery from devastation and defeat, it is the nature both of war and the human psyche that much of what remains unfinished will pass on to the next generation, in one form or another. One of these forms is self-replicating patterns of trauma which could be seen as conscious or unconscious traumatic re-enactments. A second nuclear devastation of Japan could be viewed from that perspective. As disturbing and even frightening as flashbacks may seem, they present an opportunity to discover those thoughts, feelings, hidden truths and incomplete movements which still remain fixated in space and time. Beginning with this recognition, individuals, families and entire cultures can then find a path to completion. From my perspective the US, Britain and other countries involved in the defeat and nuclear devastation of Japan will need to be involved in this process or these long fractal patterns will continue to repeat and involve all of us in (radioactive) ways that we can no longer avoid.

The UK, of course, was heavily involved in the war against Japan and also in occupation, reconstruction and then investment and promotion of nuclear power plants there. They provided fuel for these reactors and as a result, remain deeply entangled with the fate of Japan. In a British media flashback, *The Daily Mail* (March 14, 2011) ran the following headline: "The nightmare returns: Chilling echoes of Hiroshima's destruction in images from the aftermath of tsunami". The publication continues on to describe this event as Japan's worst disaster since the Second World War. Their article also published photographs juxtaposing war torn images from Hiroshima and Nagasaki with those of coastal towns flattened by a sudden upsurge and onrush of deadly tidal waves. However, it soon became apparent that this natural disaster also had a manmade nuclear component.

TRAUMA: TIME, SPACE and FRACTALS

Traumatic flashbacks and other memories of the 1945 nuclear devastation continued to increase as it gradually became known that this combination of quake and tsunami had severely crippled six aging nuclear reactors with six thousand workers still inside. The Fukushima Daiichi Nuclear Power Reactor Complex, among the largest in the world, responsible for providing a third of the nation's electricity, was totally unprepared.[47]

TRAUMA: TIME, SPACE and FRACTALS

5

FUKUSHIMA DAIICHI COMPLEX

The nuclear accident at the Fukushima Daiichi plant was like a third atomic bombing that Japan inflicted on itself.

(Kenzaburo Oe, Nobel Laureate in Literature, 1994)

While we are the victims, we are also the perpetrators.

(Haruki Murakami, novelist, June, 2011)

Honshu Island: In Japanese, *shima* means "district", and Fukushima, about half the size of Belgium, is located about 150 miles north of Toyko. The six reactor complex which rests on a campus larger than the U.S. Pentagon was built on the site of a World War II Imperial air force base. Tokyo Electric and Power Company (TEPCO), Japan's nuclear power operator, was quick to provide spokesmen to state the company line, that they

TRAUMA: TIME, SPACE and FRACTALS

believed their earthquake/tsunami catastrophe to be a *soteigai* ; a unique and unforeseeable event.

The truth is that people, and especially profit obsessed corporations, have a hard time planning for events that they don't want to happen. Nevertheless, an earthquake unleashed a wave four stories tall. This wall of water leapt over concrete barriers designed to defend against typhoons, but not earthquakes, and severely damaged the six reactors and cooling pools that prevented hot fuel rods from melting down. This allegedly unforeseen event at the Fukushima Daiichi Complex Nuclear Power Station generated a series of equipment failures; fires, three hydrogen explosions, and the world's first triple meltdown. As early as March 18th, physicist Michio Kaku warned, "a meltdown is forever".[48]

Even worse, these meltdowns were followed by a core "melt-through" of secondary containment vessels. A melt-through is a much feared and extremely dire outcome of a nuclear disaster, whereby molten nuclear lava honeycombs its containers and continues on down into the crust of the Earth. This carries a risk of further explosions and what has been called "The China Syndrome"; a situation which Uehara Haruo, architect of reactor number three, has termed "inevitable". Hiroaki Koide, Assistant Professor at Kyoto University Research Reactor Institute, explains that as the nuclear magma continues downward into the ground, superheated underground water, precariously near the surface, will create a massive hydro-volcanic explosion similar to a nuclear bomb. In view of this very real probability, the dimensions of this tragedy continue to expand. During the immediate aftermath, the number of nuclear refugees eventually grew to over eighty thousand.[49] In a humanitarian crisis of this magnitude, the eventuality of post traumatic problems is inevitable.

Now we find ourselves entering into the nightmare realm of an epic global trauma. Toward the end of 2011 it was revealed that on March 15th, reactor number three which had contained MOX plutonium fuel had exploded twice, sending 100,000 highly radioactive plutonium-rich fuel rods up into the atmosphere. Mox plutonium fuel is 2 million times more dangerous than enriched uranium and the exploded reactor had contained at least 500 lbs. of plutonium. Just one pound of evenly spread plutonium could kill everyone on our planet. Due to prevailing easterly winds and precipitation these high levels of lethal radiation soon contaminated surrounding areas including Tokyo. In an interview with *The Huffington Post,* Nuclear Engineer Akira Tokuhiro explains that since the Earth rotates counter-clockwise, most of this MOX fallout is likely to drop on the United States. In reality, this Fukushima Daiichi disaster is now contaminating our entire planetary ecosystem. Irreversibly damaged reactors continue to release radioactive particles into our biosphere, seeping into ground water, ocean currents, local landscapes and the global food chain which involves all plant and animal life. Massive quantities of radioactive materials and contaminated water from the spent fuel pools continue to flow into the Humboldt Current, familiar to the Japanese as *Kuroshio*. Also known as "the Black Stream", the *Kuroshio* is the driving force for the North Pacific Current. This relatively narrow and rapidly moving band of water is conveying a concentration of radioactive poisons around the North Pacific, across the Bering Strait to southern Alaska, Canada, and down the west coasts of the United States and Mexico.[50] Mainstream media outlets are silent and local populations remain, for the most part, unaware.

When this contaminated North Pacific Current arrives along the continental shelf, it divides. One stream veers northward along the coasts of Alaska and Canada and the breeding grounds of seals, sea otters, walruses and whales. The other stream turns south and becomes the California Current and breeding waters of sea lions, pelicans, and humpback whales. This stream, in turn, divides again into the Equatorial Pacific, moving from

Mexico to the Philippines where it rejoins the *Kuroshio* and the Peruvian heading south along the coast of South America and then westward out into the South Pacific. Mega-scale hydrodynamics reveal that this Fukushima nuclear disaster is in the process of contaminating most of the vital fisheries of the Pacific. The Pacific covers half of the planet's ocean surface. Once the radioactive and other contaminants arrive in the Southern Sea surrounding Antarctica, the poisons will continue along into the Atlantic and Indian Oceans. [51]

Meanwhile, an estimated twenty million tons of tsunami debris, swept into Pacific currents, continues on a course toward Midway Atoll, Hawaii and the west coast of North America. Polluting as it goes, this flotsam of toxic trash contains bodies, houses, cars, appliances, industrial waste, hormone disrupting polychlorinated biphenols, pesticides and plastics in a debris field estimated to be approximately 2000 miles long and 1,000 miles wide. In combination with radioactive waste, these pollutants generate a chemical stew dangerous to marine and other biological life as well as an ongoing hazard for international shipping lanes. This triple threat en route from northeast Japan carries unprecedented levels of nuclear, biological and chemical contaminants. . Radioactive cesium and strontium are already in the food chain on their way up from plankton to invertebrates like squid and then fish such as salmon, halibut and tuna. Sea animals are being exposed to tons of biological waste from pig farms and untreated sludge from the tsunami ravaged coasts of Japan. These substances are known to carry pathogens such as the avian flu virus which can affect fish and turtles, as well as humans. Chemical compounds from this massive toxic mess will eventually evaporate up into cloud formations and precipitate as rain and snowfall across the North American continent. Eventually, these nuclear, biological and chemical toxins will contaminate agricultural products, rivers, reservoirs, aquifers and well water. [52]

TRAUMA: TIME, SPACE and FRACTALS

As is the nature of corporate controlled governments and industries, both TEPCO and Japanese officials initially responded to their nuclear crisis with denial, outright lies, media control and other attempts at spin and cover-up. These all too familiar reassuring platitudes seem to be standard protocol for corporate controlled governments, intent on concealment. The excuse is more or less always the same, "we need to avoid panic". The sad result is that we are often left with a public relations success and a public health disaster. In Japan, as undeniable truths began to emerge, officials then attempted to minimize dangers of what is now known as the worst industrial accident in the history of humanity, as well as our world's most dangerous nuclear disaster. [53]

This Fukushima debacle is now being evaluated in comparison to the former USSR's April 25, 1986 Chernobyl disaster, which occurred in a land locked and relatively isolated area which is now part of Ukraine. This meltdown, from only one reactor, burned for just 10 days and permanently contaminated an immediate area of 77,000 square miles. Moreover, a radioactive plume from that single reactor extended far beyond the borders of Ukraine and "rained out" poisons resulting in lethal hot spots throughout the Northern Hemisphere. As a result, over 40% of the European land mass remains contaminated with cesium 137 and other radioactive isotopes which will concentrate in food for hundreds of thousands of years. Vast areas of Asia from Turkey to China, the United Arab Emirates, North Africa and North America have also been contaminated. All in all over 200 million people have been exposed to these poisons.

Recent research indicates that nearly a million people have lost their lives due to conditions linked to the Chernobyl disaster. These people died from cancers, congenital deformities, immune deficiencies, cardiovascular damage, endocrine abnormalities and radiation induced infant mortality. Studies conducted by Alexey Yablokov in 2000, fourteen years after the Chernobyl explosion found that only 20 % of children in the Chernobyl territories of Belarus, Ukraine and European Russia were considered "practically healthy", compared to 90 % before the disaster. This tragedy is ongoing and much remains uncertain about the longer term effects of radiation exposure. [54]

We now know that the ongoing, uncontrolled, multiple meltdowns of the Japanese reactors is far worse than Chernobyl and large areas of the country are becoming uninhabitable. One of the world's largest cities is a mere 140 miles from these fatally damaged reactors. The city water supply and sewage of Japan's capital is contaminated with increasing levels of radioactivity, and lethal hotspots are being discovered in many precincts. Britain, France, Italy and Australia have advised their citizens who are not required to be there, to leave.

At least some of government and corporate use of deceptive language and attempts to weave a polite veil of secrecy may be understood in the context of Japanese culture which is linguistically vague and averse to stating facts in an overt manner. The concept of duality is very important whereby an individual's inner *hone* self or "the truth", and their public *tatemae* self, concerned with "appearances", can be radically different. This duality is strongly encouraged in the interest of social harmony. As I understand it, in Japanese culture it is also important not to "lose face" and this can mean avoiding any responsibility which could lead to criticism, shame or loss of dignity. The Japanese axiom *uso mo hoben* translates into something like "lying is also a means to an end". Skillful lying, therefore, is commendable as something that mature adults in society must learn to do. *Tatemae*, however extends beyond white lies into the realm of what one gains by avoiding complete disclosure. When things break down and everyone is expected to lie, who or what can anyone trust? [55]

TRAUMA: TIME, SPACE and FRACTALS

Yoichi Shimatsu, former editor of *The Japan Times Weekly* and lecturer from Tsinghua University, suggests the likelihood of an agenda far more nefarious than a cultural *tatemae* of deceit. He believes that confused and bumbling responses, miscommunications and half-baked reports coming out of the Fukushima Daiichi Complex were likely driven by some unspoken factor. According to Mr. Shimatsu, the most logical explanation for this smoke and mirrors performance is that industry and government agencies are scrambling to prevent discovery of atomic bomb research facilities hidden inside Japan's civilian nuclear power plants.[56] This would not be surprising given the old adage that "one becomes what one resists". Here the history of place also has a role in this traumatic re-enactment. It is now known that during the final months of World War II, Imperial Army soldiers forced Japanese children to dig for stones containing uranium ore in Fukushima prefecture as part of Japan's efforts to manufacture an atomic weapon. The children were told, "With the stones that you boys are digging up, we can make a bomb the size of a matchbox that will destroy all of New York".[57]

Mr. Shimatsu maintains that this recent, secret nuclear weapons program is a ghost in the machine, detectable only when the system of information management and control either lapses or breaks down. He further advocates a much closer look at the gap between the official account and unexpected events and how this relates to a national security mindset. As an avid environmentalist, Yoichi Shimatsu believes that dependency upon nuclear power represents "a cult of blind faith to a fallen idol" that refuses to heed warnings from genuine science. "This nuclear cult", he believes "is as crazed and toxic as the Aum Shinriyko (terrorist cult) who unleashed a poison gas attack on the Tokyo subway; which proves again that all cults carry the seeds of their own apocalypse". [58] Despite these often transparent and suspicious sounding official evasions, at least some degree of danger was eventually acknowledged. Soon thereafter, connections with previous traumas began to emerge.

During a speech in Barcelona in June 2011, on the occasion of accepting the International Catalunya Prize, writer and translator Haruki Murakami addressed the recent tsunami and nuclear disasters. A literary superstar in his own country, Murakami is often praised as one of the world's great novelists. The processing of collective trauma has been an important theme in his work. According to Murakami, the Japanese people should have rejected nuclear power after having "learned through the sacrifice of the *hibakusha* just how badly radiation leaves scars on the world and human wellbeing". While donating the proceeds of his literary prize to the victims of the March 11th earthquake, tsunami and nuclear crisis, he offered the following:

As you know, the Japanese people are the only people in history to experience the blast of an atomic bomb. In August of 1945 atomic bombs were dropped on the

TRAUMA: TIME, SPACE and FRACTALS

cities of Hiroshima and Nagasaki from United States bombers. Over two hundred thousand people lost their lives. Almost all of the dead were unarmed civilians. But my purpose today is not to debate the pros and cons of those acts.

What I want to talk about is not only the deaths of those two hundred thousand people who died immediately after the bombing, but also the deaths over a period of time of the many who survived the bombings, those who suffered from illnesses caused by exposure to radiation. We have learned from the sacrifices of those people how destructive a nuclear weapon can be, and how deep the scars are that radiation leaves behind in this world, in the bodies of people...

There is a monument set up to pacify the spirits of those who lost their lives to the atomic bomb at Hiroshima. These are the words engraved there:

"Please rest in peace. We will not repeat this mistake."

This is a historic experience for us Japanese; our second massive nuclear disaster. But this time no one dropped a bomb on us. We set the stage, we committed the crime with our own hands, we are destroying our own lands, and we are destroying our own lives...While we are the victims, we are also the perpetrators. We must fix our eyes on this fact. If we fail to do so, we will inevitably repeat the same mistake again, somewhere else.[59]

Other images and language in Japanese, American and British vocabularies reminiscent of World War II continued to surface. This became apparent as

TRAUMA: TIME, SPACE and FRACTALS

UK papers again tuned into traumatic re-enactments now emerging on an almost daily basis. On March 19, 2011, *The Independent* published a political cartoon illustrating Japan's desperate, and ultimately futile, attempts to avert a meltdown by cooling overheated, exposed, drying reactor fuel rods with helicopter flyovers dumping seawater. One alarmed and discouraged physicist described this effort as "employing a squirt gun against a forest fire". In this cartoon, then Prime Minister Naoto Kan is cleverly drawn in the guise of a *kamikaze* pilot. He flies a rickety old World War II bomber plane emblazoned with nuclear power symbols. As Kan flies toward the radioactive reactor ruins, we see that he is armed with a single, very small bucket of water already half empty in his careless hands. Dazed, Kan turns away from his target and faces the viewing public while expressing a cry of "*Banzai!*"

These war time suicide bombing missions of *kamikaze* pilots were also evoked by the Japanese themselves who recognized that self-sacrifice was going to be called upon, once again, as a matter of national pride and survival. This tradition dates back to the honor codes of the *Samurai*, Japanese knights who followed an honor code of *Bushido* that mandates their life in service of a mission. Shortly after the meltdown crisis began, Prime Minister Kan virtually ordered nuclear workers to undertake a suicide mission into and around the now lethal reactors. He told workers that "retreat is unthinkable". While these workers were clothed in hazmat protective body suits, this gear provides slight protection against levels of radiation four times above levels known to cause cancer.

Although Japanese authorities have thrown a cloak of secrecy around these workers, according to some reports, several have already developed Acute Radiation Syndrome. Symptoms of ARS range from acute fatigue, nausea, vomiting, hair loss, hemorrhages, flu-like pain and fever leading to death. Under current conditions, Fukushima suicide workers are receiving the same amount of radiation in one hour that US nuclear personnel would be exposed to over an entire career. Don Milton, a medical doctor who specializes in occupational medicine at the Maryland Institute for Applied Environmental Health, reports that any rapid onset of ARS is an indication of very bad news. These modern day Samurai are being hailed as national heroes and sources close to them report that they are not afraid to die. Traumatic flashbacks continue in a statement issued by Keiichi Nakagawa, a professor at Tokyo University's Department of Radiology, "I don't know any other way to say it, but this is like suicide fighters in a war."[60]

And now the specter of *hibukasha* has appeared again as thousands of nuclear refugees have fled government mandated exclusion zones. While many took refuge in temporary shelters, people were turned away and also refused medical attention for fear of contamination. Before they could be admitted, evacuees were required to provide certificates confirming that they had not been exposed to radiation. Tens of thousands remain displaced and many suffer an additional burden of "survival guilt" for remaining alive and not being able to do more for those who were lost. Another wave, this time of suicides, sometimes involving entire families, is soaring in a country which already has one of the highest suicide rates in the world. Refugees who voluntarily fled Fukushima's farms, schools and fishing ports to seek safety for themselves, were accused of betrayal by those they left behind; criticized as "un-Japanese" and also shunned as potentially radioactive. This situation is further complicated by the fact that the issue of safety from radiation is not at all clear and trust in local and national authorities is waning. [61]

Adding to steadily increasing levels of anxiety, the Japanese government has now revealed that civilians living in areas not being evacuated are expected to receive doses up to 23 times higher than annual legal limits over a course of this next year and on into an extended period of time. This may be something of an understatement given the massive levels of radioactive particles still being unleashed into air, earth, food and water. More than one nuclear expert now foresees a likelihood that most of northern Japan is becoming uninhabitable and the seismic future of their entire archipelago is in doubt. How painfully ironic that this culture which virtually forbids any and all immigration, may find that their best option for survival may be to become immigrants themselves.

As of now, our Southern Hemisphere has been less impacted by radiation, and Japanese people already have successful communities in Latin America. I have had the pleasure of working with some of these people in Peru. Many of the Japanese over here in the New World are descendants of those who fled after the bombing of Hiroshima and Nagasaki.

TRAUMA: TIME, SPACE and FRACTALS

While it is natural for traumatized individuals and entire populations to experience flashbacks to previous and unresolved traumas, an important step in individual and social trauma recovery is to recognize both similarities, and more importantly differences in past and present time. Japan of 2011 is not the same as Japan of 1945. Re-building radioactive sites of flood and nuclear devastation is contraindicated by the omnipresence of cesium, strontium, plutonium and other isotopes which have likely rendered these areas permanently uninhabitable. The good news is that, at present, more is known about the dangers of radiation exposure, symptoms of acute and long term exposure, as well as options for prevention and treatment. As a result one could hope that the fate of this latest generation of *hibakusha* will be more enlightened. Through no fault of their own, these men, women and children must now find a way to live with uncertainty, a sense of taint, fear of radiation effects, of being inwardly poisoned and being carriers of mutant genes that could be lethal to subsequent generations. Activist Keiko Ichikawa reports that huge numbers of malformed Japanese babies are already being quietly aborted so they will not be seen. [62]

Economic recovery will present new challenges as one of the world's strongest economies now finds its exports unwelcome and under suspicion of radioactive contamination. These new challenges of 2011 will require new ways of finding individual and community resources. In an effort to raise the spirits of Fukushima area residents, as well as lighten the impact of radiation, Koyu Abe, chief monk at the Buddhist Joenji temple began to grow sunflowers and other healing plants.

We plant sunflowers, field mustard, amaranthus and cockscomb, which are all believed to absorb radiation. So far we have grown at least 200,000 flowers (at this temple) and distributed many more seeds".

Unfortunately, the question remains of what to do with all of these radioactive flowers which have since proved to be of little value in de-contamination efforts. Nevertheless, over 100 volunteers assist with this project which includes lighting candles and burning papers inscribed with names of the dead. This ritual is believed to symbolically "reunite" departed spirits with their neighborhood. Abe also believes that by taking action, his volunteers could help locals to shake off a sense of stagnation and find hope. He counsels:

> To overcome this disaster, we should accept that it has already happened and face the reality. Then we should pursue what we can do at this very moment, what impact we can make and how each one of us can diligently work to improve the situation. [63]

This very wise and trauma savvy monk has found a way to gently acknowledge the past and also bring survivors into immediate healing moments of a purposeful *now*. It could also be that a collective level of Japanese social trauma recovery may require a willingness to take a fresh look at their interdependent relationship with the United States, our allies and a shared belief in this myth of nuclear energy as an eco-friendly, clean, safe source of energy. While the question remains as to how that could be accomplished...do we still have a choice when the alternative is already here? And maybe it's already too late ...as legendary songwriter Bob Dylan wrote, at what now seems a long time ago... "The answer, my friend, is blowin' in the wind... the answer is blowin' in the wind". Poetic, yes and that was then and this is now, and those of us still here, still have a choice.

Now, twenty five years after the handwriting appeared on the deserted walls of Chernobyl, we must again ask ourselves: "Why is nuclear power still viable in view of these catastrophic accidents? What could possibly justify the huge financial outlays, weapons proliferation, environmental devastation, and nuclear waste epidemics of cancers, other lethal diseases, and genetic damage continuing on to future generations?" There is, of course, the reality of the fortunes to be made by the few. Also, many government officials, and paid-for politicians still pitch the government sponsored, nuclear industry slogan of: the safe, clean and green alternative to fossil fuels. The increasing dangers of proliferation will continue as long as the public remains in the dark as to the multiple risks of radiation exposure. Despite the claims of the military/industrial/corporate complex, nuclear power is not our best option. The truth is that numerous, non-nuclear, cost-effective, people and planet friendly solutions have long been available through alternative technologies.

For Japan, however, any such a realization may be already too late. By January 2012 the diaspora was already underway. According to *Yomimuri Shinbun* (January 5, 2012) the Japanese government/industrial complex has developing plans to build a new "Small Japan" in the southern Indian township of Chennai for the benefit of 50,000 residents. This new 'eco-friendly" city will include a "Japanese quality" infrastructure, industrial park, seaside resort, hospital, shopping mall and golf course.

Industrial plants housed within this new region are expected to be operational by 2013. And indeed, the *Times of India* (January 11, 2012) has reported that the Tamil Nadu government has signed a memorandum of understanding for the location and construction of this new 1,500 acre "Japan Town". "It's all about money" said Dr. Haruki Madarame, of Japan's Nuclear Safety Commission, "whether 'it' is about a nuclear power plant, a nuclear waste facility or a Japanese-only city in southern India." Critics have likened this project to a post-apocalyptic, post-nuclear reality with a safe haven community for the select from government and industry. The corporate elite should feel quite at home there since India's first fast breed nuclear reactor will be built just 70 km south of Chennai. The elderly, infirm and especially the outcast *hibakusha* will have no place in this luxurious new settlement. (http://ex-skfblogspot.com). In the interim, many of the privileged have sent their loved ones to Singapore and other less radioactive locales.

Less elitist "people to people" evacuation efforts are being undertaken by donor supported web sites such as Iori Mochizuki's *Fukushima Diary,* which lists addresses and organizations from the international community willing to assist Japanese, their families and loved ones in the challenging process of finding new homes in less radioactive parts of the world. ("Evacuate": http://fukushima-diary.com).

6

THE CRANE

By late spring of 2011 it was clear, to me at least, that the situation in Japan was becoming increasingly grave for their entire population, their neighbors and our whole planet. This, however, was not reflected in our major mainstream media. After the initial coverage of the crisis in March, Japan was relegated to the back pages or dropped altogether. Most of my sources are from the internet, alternative media and foreign media outlets. As I see it, the most obvious reason for a near black out of Fukushima news is that many corporations such as GE and Westinghouse that are invested in these nuclear power plants are also heavily invested in networks such as CBS and MSNBC. The nuclear power industry has close ties with government, and media and information coming out of Japan presents a serious challenge to both the myth of safety and their current and projected profits.

Unfortunately, many assume that anything not being covered by mainstream news is either not happening, or irrelevant. The general impression here in America is that the Fukushima accident has already been taken care of and that is why it is no longer in our news. Others who might acknowledge that something serious might have happened don't see why it would have anything to do with them...after all Japan is so far away. It is also true, that there are those who just don't care or don't want to know about anything that they feel that they can't do anything about.

Early in May I travelled to Germany to attend an international systemic conference. Lilacs were in full bloom in a glorious Bavarian spring and there were about one hundred of us attending from all over the world. I look forward to these seasonal gatherings to commune with former teachers, colleagues, friends, and also to learn what's new in our international work. Given the severity of the crisis in Japan I wondered if any of our Japanese colleagues would be able to attend. At the first plenary session I noticed three women and a man from Japan sitting in a back row towards the exit. They were looking quite lost and initially seemed to prefer to remain at some distance from the rest of the group. When I thought about approaching them, I was overcome by an immense, almost paralyzing sadness. Researching replicating patterns of social trauma in Japan is one thing, but facing these Japanese people, for me, was quite another experience. At the time I felt that it would not be helpful to add my sense of overwhelm to theirs. It could also be that I carry some modicum of collective guilt for the nuclear devastation of 1945. In this respect, it has been somewhat helpful to recall an experience shared by one peace activist who found herself overwhelmed by both grief and guilt at a war memorial in Hiroshima. Her Japanese guide only chuckled, "Don't worry", he said, "If we had had this atomic bomb we would have dropped it on you". Yes perhaps, and the fact remains that they did not drop it on us, we dropped it on them.

During another morning plenary, a German facilitator, Sneh Victoria Schnabel announced that she had been requested to offer a half day workshop on the subject of the situation in Japan. She works with trauma and systemic constellation work, often in group settings. I was relieved and hopeful that some attention would now be given to this massive social and now global trauma. There were about 50 of us in Sneh's workshop from many different countries and cultures. She began, as she often does, by just checking in with participants in a round. As each person spoke it became clear that there was an enormous resistance to our topic of Japan. Some expressed a desire to use this group's time to work on their own individual traumas, or of incidents that had happened in the workplace. Others spoke of resentment and even some anger that this topic had been chosen over others such as Iraqi suicide bombers or Brazilian street children. I know many people in this group to be sensitive and tuned-in individuals who are actively engaged in the healing and helping professions. In retrospect, I wonder if on this occasion they were picking up on and reflecting an even wider international field of many others, who for a variety of reasons, do not wish to acknowledge either the pain or danger of the Fukushima meltdowns.

Being in groups like this is sometimes uncomfortable for me because I am something like an empath and this can mean that I find myself feeling what others are unwilling or unable to experience. As this group energy hardened, I looked over at one of the Japanese ladies, who was struggling to hold back silent tears running down her cheeks. As she softly returned my gaze I started to cry with overwhelming waves of uncontrollable grief, far deeper than any words could possibly express. Sneh had clearly determined that this event was to be about Japan and not anyone person's individual issue. She trusts The Field and I felt secure in the feeling that she would stay on message. I have seen her work before and admire her skill in managing resistance, overwhelm and cross culturally sensitive issues. After the check in, she stood and invited the whole group to form a circle, which would form for the purpose of offering a container to gently surround anyone in need of support.

The terrible grief was not subsiding and I quickly moved toward the center of this gathering and stood there helplessly weeping. My feeling now was that there was no longer any personal "me", only this seemingly endless sorrow that had something to do with "man's inhumanity to man". Many others with personal issues, not related to our topic, stepped briefly into this circle but when asked if they needed to remain stepped back into the larger circle. And then slowly, shyly, one of the Japanese ladies looked for permission to Sneh, who nodded in the affirmative. She then tentatively entered an outer edge of our circle, and a second woman followed. A third, much younger Japanese lady slipped in as well and stood by her side. In a single elegant gesture, the younger lady lifted her silk shawl up over her head and body and sank to the floor in what appeared to be a posture of shame and defeat. There was something iconic, almost archetypal, in her gesture of the vanquished that was incredibly painful to witness. It was clear that a powerful, healing resource was needed. Sneh called for a volunteer to serve as a representative for the Eternal Soul of Japan, which she acknowledged as being very, very old. A strong woman stepped forward and took up a position facing these two women. When this representative arrived, I felt that it was time for me to step back into the larger circle.

The room was silent. The Eternal Soul felt that she had become a column of light, and that she was sending that light to the three women. (Later she reported that while she could both see and feel their pain, it didn't adhere to her). She addressed the Japanese man still standing in the outer circle and said that it would be best for him to join the women. As two of the women looked toward him, one said that they would all feel better if he would join them and he took his place to their right. At this point, the third, younger lady lifted her shawl, looked up at the "Japanese Soul" and was able to stand. The representative of the Japanese Soul reported that she felt as though she had symbols in her hands and asked if she might approach each of the Japanese people and place these symbols in their hearts by laying her hands on their upper chests. Slowly, each agreed. While this was happening, another representative came in and stood behind the Eternal Soul. This was an energy from a higher level, beyond right or wrong or good or evil. The four nodded and the man looked at her hands and said that he saw a crane, the national bird of Japan. As these three looked at the Japanese Soul my tears began to ebb. Now I felt as though I could breathe again and trust that the Japanese people would find their own collective ways of facing yet another life threatening challenge.

During a lunch break I noticed that our Japanese colleagues were actively engaged in conversations with other participants and we briefly exchanged smiles. "So nice to see you smiling", I said, and they replied "Oh, yes, and you too!" Later in the day, the Japanese man approached the woman who had represented the Japanese Soul and asked to see her ring. This simple gold band was etched with delicate wings, "wings of Isis", she explained. He nodded, and still we all knew that the important thing was that he had "seen" a crane. In Japanese culture the crane is a beloved symbol of honor, peace, loyalty and longevity. Cranes, the tallest and most elegant of all flying birds, are members of the *Gruidae* family. The Japanese variety are called *tancho* meaning "red crown" and stand nearly five feet tall. The circle of bright red skin on their heads, and snow white feathers with black markings are also colors of the Japanese flag, and cranes have a prominent role as important symbols in art and craft.

The Japanese crane was once widespread over much of their country. Unfortunately, cranes sustained heavy losses during World War II and the subsequent occupation. In 1952 the government supported the feeding of surviving cranes and these graceful birds were able to return from the brink of extinction. In this way, they also serve as a poignant reminder of the Japanese capacity for resilience. The Japanese have a mystical folk belief that since cranes "live for a thousand years" folding a thousand paper cranes can grant longevity and cure one of illness. The origin of these origami cranes and their correspondence to healing the wounds of nuclear devastation can now be traced back more than five decades.

Sadako Sasaki was exposed to the atomic bomb in Hiroshima at the age of two. For the next ten years she developed into an apparently healthy, happy, bright and vigorously athletic girl. And then she developed swellings on her neck, behind her ears and purple spots appeared on her legs. Sadoko was diagnosed with leukemia resulting from delayed radiation effects and given less than a year to live. Her story has since become something of a legend, which says that she struggled to stay alive by folding one crane after another in hopes of making the legendary thousand. Some of these origami cranes were actually made from her blood reports, and medicine wrappings which she hung from the ceiling above her bed. Sadako's mother whispered a poem over each folded paper bird that she used to recite when her daughter was young: "Oh, flock of heavenly cranes, cover my child with your wings". It is said that Sadako completed 644, still 356 short of the necessary thousand. The story continues that her classmates added the missing number so that a full thousand could be placed in her coffin. After her death, a national campaign began in order to raise funds for a monument dedicated to Sadako and all other children killed by the atomic bombs. Financial contributions accompanied by paper cranes arrived from all over Japan. This monument now stands near the center of Hiroshima's peace park, topped by a statue of Sadako holding a golden crane.[64]

A focus group formed around this story, *Orizuru No Kai,* or the Folded Crane Club. This children's group is led by Ichiro Kawamoto, a day laborer who has involved himself in antinuclear activities of every kind. His children's group visits hospitals to help and sometimes serve as family for Atomic bomb patients, greets international visitors with leis of paper cranes and corresponds with children all over the world about the dangers of radiation.

7

BLIND SPOT

We have genuflected before the god of science only to find that it has given us the atomic bomb, producing fears and anxieties that science can never mitigate.

Martin Luther King Jr.

While I believe that a knowledge of relationship and family dynamics is an important component of systemically oriented trauma work, I have come to understand that it is also important to consider the social, political, religious, historical, environmental and other factors that contribute to the shape of any system. I have not always known this and at the beginning of my practice there were still many blind spots, some personal and others cultural, which obscured an appreciation of the significance of these external factors. In retrospect, this is now clear as I recall issues presented by Rachel and Jack, a childless couple in early middle age who were having relationship difficulties. Rachel cried throughout most of our first session all the while saying that she wasn't sure why. When I gently inquired as to what might be the saddest thing in her life, she replied, "my marriage". Then, as something like an afterthought she mentioned that the couple had 13 cats that all died of *leukemia*. In hindsight, this apparent afterthought was an essential window into much deeper issues that neither I nor they understood at the time.

Rachel believed that "something was terribly wrong" in her marriage but she had no idea what that might be since it appeared that she and Zack got along well. She went on to explain that she had no idea either as to why they married or had remained together for over ten years. I asked if she would be willing to offer a description of their wedding since information about marriage ceremonies often provides insight into a relationship and its prognosis. Rachel and Zack were married on Halloween, with an all chocolate wedding cake, bride, groom and all their guests wore black.

Clearly there had been a pall over this marriage from the onset, with no idea as to the nature of this darkness. With considerable reluctance, Zack attended a few sessions, and steadfastly insisted that there was nothing amiss in their marriage. He wanted to make it clear, that above all, he loved Rachel and would continue to love her, as long as he lived. Eventually they divorced.

Decades later, and years after retiring from private practice, I received a long letter from Rachel informing me of Zack's death and of the circumstances surrounding his demise. As we re-established contact, and with new information, we were finally able to arrive at some clarity and a deeper understanding of the powerful external forces that had shaped this troubling relationship. As it turned out, Rachel's father had been one of the scientists involved in the Manhattan Project which developed our first nuclear weapons. While involved in chemical engineering projects at a well-known Radiation Laboratory, his family knew only that he worked in a "radiator factory."

During Zack's service in the Navy he was one of many thousands who were set up by our military, under orders, to serve as witnesses to nuclear testing events in the South Pacific. While stationed at Christmas Island he was among those ordered to witness multiple tests of both atomic and hydrogen bombs. Near the end of his life, Zack began to tell Rachel about his naval service in the Pacific Proving Grounds. He hadn't shared any of these experiences during their marriage because he didn't think the subject important and also couldn't see that his military history had anything whatsoever to do with their relationship. As Rachel sadly listened, Zack began to recall that our troops were given Geiger counters and then instructed to throw them away. Multiple detonations were witnessed by thousands without protective gear. Most of these (sacrificial) military personnel were outfitted in nothing more than sunglasses, sandals and bathing trunks. Zack told Rachel that he was comfortably clad in a sarong.

Zack married again, a friend of Rachel's and they stayed in touch. Around that time he had a malignant melanoma removed from his back, and slowly began to connect the dots between his massive degree of radiation exposure and his cancer. The new couple began to attend meetings at their local chapter of the National Radiation Survivors Association. This non-profit organization was founded in 1982 in order to promote education about the long term effects of exposure to radioactive substances. These meetings, designed to connect and support, soon became increasingly depressing as fewer veterans were showing up and attendees were now mostly mothers, widows and surviving children. The newlyweds soon realized that many of these absent members were also Atomic Veterans who had met an early demise from *leukemia* and other forms of radiation induced cancers. Zack's second marriage didn't last and he quickly endeavored to resume a close friendship with Rachel. While his devotion was somewhat puzzling for her, Zack continued to maintain that he would love her until the day he died. After his cancer was finally diagnosed as terminal, he shot himself in the head with a pistol his uncle had brought back from World War II. Zack didn't share his plans with Rachel because suicide is a crime in their state and he didn't want her to be charged as an accomplice. He also made an attempt to protect her from some of the shock by making prior arrangements for notification and follow up.

Neither Zack nor any other of the 500,000 Atomic Veterans, were ever compensated for exposure to lethal doses of radiation. Our Defense Department and Pentagon did not permit any mention of atomic test participation on their military discharge forms. In addition, our Defense Department had demanded that most military personnel swear an oath of secrecy, under penalty of imprisonment, if they were to mention in any way their association with or participation in any nuclear weapons test. Upon the one occasion when Zack applied to the Veterans Administration for benefits, he was denied because he served during the Korean Conflict which was "not a war". One now wonders what other crimes and outright atrocities may have been committed against our own loyal soldiers in the name of national security and scientific research.

Only now, from a systemic perspective has it become clear that Rachel and Zack, who presented with unknown relationship difficulties, were deeply entangled within a thermonuclear trauma bond. This couple was unable to extricate themselves because both were unaware of the significance of the fact that Rachel's father had a prominent role in creating nuclear weapons that eventually sealed Zack's fate. Unfortunately, being unaware does not protect anyone from the generational consequences of perpetrator/victim dynamics. With this new information and expanded perspective, Rachel says that she has reached some modicum of peace. She now lives on a property that Zack lovingly bequeathed to her. In her life now, she enjoys visits from a daughter from a previous marriage and several grandchildren. Rachel is pleased to report that all of her cats are also doing well and are expected to enjoy a long and healthy life.

Radiation represents a major blind spot in couples counseling, family therapy and social trauma work as well. Recent events at the Fukushima Daiichi complex, and our military's ongoing use of depleted uranium, insure that this issue will not go away. Rachel and Zack are certainly not the only couple to endure the hidden presence of nuclear radiation within their relationship. It actually defined their dynamic from the onset, and on until the final, probably inevitable, outcome.

The role of the atomic bomb in relationships and family systems has been clearly demonstrated by Bert Hellinger using his Systemic Constellation method. In this modality when seminar participants are chosen to represent members of a system, they begin to access information about the lives, relationships and feelings of those they represent. While the reason for this has never been satisfactorily explained, this phenomenon has been repeatedly observed in constellations in many vastly different cultures throughout the world. In a session conducted at a couples' workshop in Washington DC, the importance of the bomb was not immediately apparent.

The client was an American woman who stated only that she did not feel supported by her husband and that he was unwilling to do things for her, like attend this workshop. Hellinger chose a male representative for her husband. As this representative stood in silence, his body language clearly indicated an intense fear. Hellinger asked the woman, "Are you dangerous"? She appeared puzzled and after a long pause said that she didn't know. And so, Hellinger posed a second question, "Did you ever think about killing him", and this time she slowly nodded in the affirmative. "You *are* dangerous" Hellinger said, "and now we have to find out why". He asked what happened in her family, especially anything to do with murder. The client said that she had no information about anything like that and so the session was terminated at that point.

After the break, the previous session was resumed because new information that the client hadn't considered important had come to light. Her father had been one of the nuclear scientists who worked on the atomic bomb at the Los Alamos laboratory and her husband is Japanese. When asked if she was a "father's daughter", the client said no but she had longed to be his favorite. Hellinger then set up a representative for her father, another for the atomic bomb, and a group of others to represent victims of a nuclear explosion in Japan. These victims quickly gathered together alongside the Japanese husband. Her father looked only at The Bomb, which was represented by a very tall man dressed in gray, who looked over the heads of all others. The Bomb remained immobile and was just there emitting an enormous sense of presence and power. Hellinger placed the client in this constellation and she slowly gravitated toward her father who continued to look only at The Bomb.

Hellinger instructed her father to say to The Bomb "I am proud of you", the father nodded in affirmation, and then "I am proud of death". At this point, Hellinger guided the client so that she stood next to The Bomb. This, she said, "felt good". Now, it became clear that as her father looked again, he could now finally see her when she stood next to The Bomb. "You see", Hellinger observed, "she is identified with The Bomb". Next, one of the Japanese victims collapsed to the floor and began writhing as if in unimaginable agony. The husband was drawn to her side and made increasingly futile attempts to comfort her. Upon seeing this, the client moved slowly away from The Bomb, toward her husband and the agonized victim, and then fell to her knees before them and grieved. Soon afterward, the victim was able to lie quiet, as if "finally dead".

The Bomb remained impassive and the father remained apart from this scene with fists clenched in aggression. Hellinger chose another male representative and placed him behind the father. He then turned the father around to face this new representative and told him to tell this man "I did my duty". This, Hellinger explained, is the statement of an obedient child to a parent, and the underlying dynamic of those who unquestioningly follow orders. Hellinger went on to point out that those who had created The Bomb attributed the same qualities to this weapon that they imagined were also possessed by God…to create and destroy. (I have become Shiva….) "Those", he said, "Who employ these weapons feel God-like in their power". This, in part, explains the ongoing attraction to nuclear power despite all the known and unknown dangers to life itself.

TRAUMA: TIME, SPACE and FRACTALS

On other occasions, Bert Hellinger has stated that The Bomb joins the family system. I have also found this to be the case in my recent experience with systemically oriented trauma work. During a seminar that I offered in Lima, Peru, which has a long standing and substantial Japanese community, a seemingly pleasant young lady asked if we could look at the source of an anger that had become problematic in her life. She described this anger as sudden, explosive and destructive. I asked if anyone else in her family had this explosive anger and she replied that several of the women on her mother's side of the family shared this trait. Inquiring further into her family history she explained that she was half-Japanese. Her father was Brazilian and her mother Japanese and that mother's family had emigrated from Japan after World War II. In asking from where in Japan her mother's family had emigrated, I felt that I already knew the answer. And yes, they came from Hiroshima.... And so, the fact that sudden, explosive, destructive anger was the presenting symptom made complete sense from a systemic perspective. I set up a representative for the client, her mother, her grandmother, Hiroshima and The Bomb. It was obvious that The Bomb had the most power in this situation and its representative immediately moved to the center of the room. Now it became clear to the others that they needed to arrange themselves in relation to this powerful entity. The representative for Hiroshima slowly moved to a place directly in front of The Bomb and announced that they belonged together. The grandmother soon followed and placed herself directly in front of the bombed city. Now, the mother took her place in front of the grandmother and the client's representative moved to a place in front of the mother.

The tableau now appeared as a direct line of power; The Bomb, Hiroshima, Grandmother, Mother and client's representative. I asked how the client's representative was feeling and she replied "peaceful". It felt safe enough now to ask the client to take her own place in the constellation and she confirmed a feeling of "peaceful". This was also confirmed by her mother and grandmother. Hiroshima and The Bomb seemed content in accepting the reality that they now belong together and acknowledging this brings a feeling of quiet. As strange as it may seem, it does appear that where the role and power of The Bomb is denied, symptoms appear in *both* the families of those who unleashed nuclear weapons and the families of those who suffered the subsequent wrath of destruction.

8

THE NUCLEAR FAMILY

There is no danger.

(Atomic Energy Commission)

The unleashed power of the atom has changed everything Except our mode of thinking and thus we drift toward unparalleled catastrophe.

(Albert Einstein, May 24, 1946)

According to science writer William L. Laurence, the Atomic Age began at exactly 5:30 AM Mountain War Time on the morning of July 15, 1945 along a stretch of New Mexico wasteland, just 21 days before Hiroshima. For Laurence the success of this nuclear test explosion at the Trinity test site was something beyond wonderful. Years later, Stuart Udall, former U.S. Secretary of the Interior, was not so convinced. "The Atomic Age", Udall wrote, "was born in secrecy, and for two decades, high priests of the cult of the atom concealed vital information about the risks to human health posed by radiation". [65]

Here it is important to bear in mind the fact that between 1946 and 1962 the United States detonated just over a thousand nuclear warheads, hurling countless tons of radioactive fallout into our atmosphere. Also here we find an all too familiar story of denial by those who profit, of any toxic chemical, petro-chemical, pharmaceutical, or atomic poison.

In *The Life and Times of the Thunderbolt Kid,* American humorist Bill Bryson recounts experiences of growing up in a post war era when ordinary folks were charmed and captivated, transfixed actually, by the broiling majesty and unnatural light of atomic bombs. For Bryson, his beloved Fifties was a schizophrenic era equally shaped by an atmosphere of wild optimism and rampant fear. I have clear memories of this time as well; the Korean Conflict was raging, McCarthyism was rampant and anyone opposed to nuclear testing was probably a "pinko commie" sympathizer.....or worse. Bryson recalls a time when our military started testing weapons in the Nevada desert outside of Las Vegas and this became the desert town's hottest tourist attraction. Within these comic recollections lies the obverse of something much darker.

People flocked to Las Vegas to stand on the desert's edge, feel the ground tremble beneath their feet, and watch the air above fill with billowing pillars of smoke and hot particle dust. These enthusiastic visitors could stay at the Atomic Motel, consume Atomic Cocktails (equal parts vodka, brandy and champagne with a splash of sherry), dine on Atomic Hamburgers, get an Atomic Hairdo, and watch the crowning of Miss Atom Bomb. Not to be missed were nightly gyrations of a stripper who called herself "The Atomic Blast".

As many as four explosions a month were carried out during these peak years in Nevada. While mushroom clouds were visible from any parking lot in the city, most tourists preferred to drive out toward an edge of the blast zone, often with picnic supplies, to watch the show and then enjoy the fallout afterwards. Radioactive dust drifted across Las Vegas, leaving clearly visible traces on nearly every surface. To add to the excitement, official looking government technicians, clad in white lab coats, appeared with Geiger counters. Patriotic citizens were all too willing and eager to line up in order to find out how radioactive they were. The mind boggles at the tragic red, white and blue naiveté of those nuclear tourists, so trusting of their government, their military and the futuristic wonders of anything atomic. We now know, and too late for many, that our government's priorities were absolutely clear; public health was secondary to "national security". Their position is reflected in Atomic Energy Commissioner Thomas Murray's unequivocal, crystal clear statement "...we must not let anything interfere with these tests, nothing!" Yes of course, *nothing,* no-one, and no living thing, animal, plant or human must stand in the way of the progress of this new weapon of mass destruction.[66] Who exactly agreed to these priorities?

Although Bill Bryson's memoirs were written toward the end of the 20th century, not much has changed for the Las Vegas of this 21st century which continues to promote atomic tourism. The tourist friendly nuclear circus came around again in 2005 with the opening of their Atomic Testing Museum. This popular facility features an interactive event in Ground Zero Theater, a bunker replica where spectators can enjoy a 10 minute video of an atomic explosion; a multisensory experience featuring thunderous sound effects, blasts of hot air and vibrating seats. Gift shop souvenirs include a fetching set of atomic bomb earrings exquisitely fashioned after the Fat Man and Little Boy bombs dropped on Japan in 1945.

Although Bryson professes to love science, he has had no difficulty in resisting any promise of a peaceful atom. Among his reasons, he cites the peacetime plans of "semi-crazed" Hungarian-born physicist Edward Teller, an early member of the Manhattan Project and one of the presiding geniuses over the development of our hydrogen bomb. Also known as the "father" of the hydrogen bomb, Teller was also generally considered to be the model for the character "Dr. Strangelove" in the 1964 movie by the same name, now a cult film classic.

Teller and his acolytes at the Atomic Energy Commission envisioned the use of their new H-bomb to create massive civil engineering projects on a scale never before imagined. They were keen to advocate open pit mines where mountains had once stood, altering the course of rivers, (insuring for instance, that the Danube only served capitalist countries) and blasting away impediments to commerce and shipping, such as Australia's Great Barrier Reef. Teller's team were especially enthusiastic about a plan to place 26 nuclear bombs in a chain across the Isthmus of Panama to widen the canal and provide quite a show in the bargain. Moreover, they suggested that nuclear devices could be used to alter Earth's weather by adjusting the amount of dust in our atmosphere. Better still, Teller suggested that we might use our only Moon as a giant target for testing nuclear warheads. Briefly then, these brilliant creators of the hydrogen bomb were eagerly looking forward to wrapping our world in unpredictable levels of radiation. In so doing they also thought it profitable to obliterate whole ecosystems and possibly our only celestial satellite and to deface the surface of the planet while antagonizing enemies and potential enemies at every given opportunity. [67]

At this point, one is torn between laughter and tears. While these Strangelovian follies may seem quite amusing, a closer look at the widespread human suffering generated by this heedlessness is quite another story. The truth is that here in the USA we have our own *hibakusha* also known as "downwinders". These are individuals and communities exposed to radioactive contamination or nuclear fallout resulting from atmospheric or underground weapons testing and nuclear accidents. Downwinders are also those individuals and communities exposed to ionizing radiation and other emissions due to the production and maintenance of nuclear weapons, nuclear power and nuclear waste. In areas located near nuclear sites, downwinders were repeatedly exposed to releases of radioactive materials into our environment, contaminating the air, topsoil, ground water systems, and food chain. Other downwinders may have suffered from exposure to uranium mines and nuclear experimentation.

Adverse immediate and long term effects from radiation exposure include acute radiation sickness, a rise in infant mortality, genetic and birth defects, cardiovascular diseases, neurological and immune suppressed disorders, as well as an increased incidence of cancers. Leukemia is often one of the first of these cancers to appear, then thyroid and later a wide variety of solid tumor malignancies.

Some of these dangers to public health began to attract public attention in 1980. *People Magazine* disclosed the alarming fact that of the 220 members of the cast and crew of the 1956 movie *The Conqueror,* who spent three months on location filming near St. George Utah, 91 had been diagnosed with cancer. That's 41%! Of these 91, 46 had died of cancer by 1980 - including the film's main stars, Susan Hayward, Agnes Moorehead, Dick Powell, John Hoyt, Pedro Armendariz and John Wayne. Back in 1955, any danger from radioactivity was considered to be a joke. Children often accompanied their parents on the movie set and Wayne and his two handsome bare chested sons were happy to pose for a photo-op featuring the three listening to a Geiger counter. Michael and Patrick Wayne also developed cancer later in life. What later became known as the "RKO Radioactive

TRAUMA: TIME, SPACE and FRACTALS

Picture" was filmed in Snow Canyon, Utah only 37 miles from the Nevada Test Site. [68]

Pro-nuclear skeptics deny that these cancers were radiation related in view of the fact that so many of this cast and crew were heavy smokers. Smoking however, does not explain the fact that over half of the nearby population of St. George also developed cancer. Not only do these people not smoke, most of the forty-five hundred citizens were known to be clean living, socially and politically conservative, patriotic Mormons who avoided coffee, tea, and all forms of tobacco and alcohol. Prior to nuclear testing, St. George and other orderly, small town Mormon communities had a low incidence of cancer. Elmer Pickett, a St. George business owner told Utah Senator Orrin Hatch, "In my own family we have nine carcinoma victims, beginning with my wife who died of cancer and leukemia combined; my niece, 5 years old, from leukemia and cancer; a sister; sister-in-law,; a mother-in-law, an uncle, a grandmother, and two other uncles".[69] No one bothered to look into the health of the hundreds of Native Americans who had served as extras in this film.

Utah native, conservationist, activist and downwinder Terry Tempest Williams tells the story of her "nuclear" family in *Refuge: An Unnatural History of Family and Place* (Pantheon, 1991) which begins with the prologue: "Most of the women in my family are dead. At thirty-four I became the matriarch of my family." In the epilogue she writes:

> I belong to The Clan of One- Breasted Women. My mother, my grandmothers and six aunts have all had mastectomies. Seven are dead. The two who survive just completed rounds of chemotherapy and radiation.
>
> I've had my own problems: two biopsies for breast cancer and a small tumor between my ribs diagnosed as "borderline malignancy". [70]

The author recounts a conversation with her father shortly after he had returned from St. George. Over dessert, she shared a recurring dream that she had for as long as she could remember in which she saw a flash of light, in the night, illuminating the desert landscape. "You, did see it", her father replied, "the bomb and then the cloud".... "In fact," he offered, "I remember the day, September 7, 1957". When Terry was a very small child, her family had been driving back from California, north past Las Vegas. An hour or so before dawn there was an enormous explosion which they all heard and felt. Their young family then witnessed a golden stemmed cloud – the iconic mushroom billowing up from the desert floor. Overhead, the night sky appeared to vibrate with an eerie pink glow. A few minutes later, light ash rained down onto their car. What she thought was a dream eventually turned into a family nightmare.

This flash of eerie light was part of operation Plumbbob, one of our government's most intensive series of nuclear test explosions. As she stared at her father in astonishment, he simply said, "I thought you knew; it was a common appearance in the Fifties." It was very common indeed.[71]

TRAUMA: TIME, SPACE and FRACTALS

During the 1950's, our nuclear cowboys unleashed at least 100 atomic sunbursts that would color early morning skies over the southwestern deserts of Nevada, Utah and Arizona, exposing every living thing to unprecedented levels of radioactivity. Radioactive ash contaminated countless wells and cisterns along with bead-like particles – the remains of atomized steel detonating towers. Hundreds and thousands of livestock and unknown numbers of wildlife sickened and died. Other casualties included hundreds, maybe thousands of conscripts that our military ordered out to the desert to serve as witnesses to these tests, "in order to observe the psychological effects of simulated nuclear warfare".[72]

A fifth generation Mormon and nature historian, Terry Tempest Williams has twice testified before Congress about Women's Health and links between environmental toxins and cancer. Cancer in her family, however, was not limited to women. She has now lost uncles to malignancies; her father has been diagnosed with prostate cancer, and her beloved younger brother Stephen died of lymphoma in 2005. While he was undergoing chemotherapy, six months before his passing, they were sitting in the hospital and Stephen looked at her and said, "I would give anything to know what mother was thinking before she died". Williams replied, "there are clues" and he nodded, "I know, *Refuge;* I never read it". Soon after, Stephen checked into Commonweal, a cancer retreat center where he finally read her book. In an emotional telephone call to his older sister, he simply said, "How could you have known twenty-years ago that you were writing this book for me?" In a recent interview Williams said that writing and her connection to Nature has been an ongoing resource. Her books, she says, don't belong to her. They just have their own life in the world – like water.

In another interview, Stephen's question of their mother's feelings about her cancer, this disease in her family and her own impending death resurfaced as something of a mystery. As she was dying, Terry's mother Diane Dixon Tempest, well known as a very private person, confided that she had kept journals and that she wanted to leave them all to Terry. Her only condition was that they would not be opened until after she passed. After her mother was gone, a collection of carefully bound, beautiful, fabric covered journals were found. Finally, the dutiful daughter found some private time to carefully explore her mother's journals. Slowly she discovered that each and every one was totally blank.[73] While the true meaning of these empty pages may never be known, a systemic perspective might shed some light. I have a theory that what one does for a living or practices as a serious hobby has something to do with unfinished and possibly hidden business of previous generations.

In *The Clan of the One-Breasted Women,* the women of the Tempest family clan and their local Mormon community were described as stoic, God-fearing, patriotic Americans who graciously bowed to the subtle constraints imposed by the patriarchy. Cancer was just part of life. In Mormon culture of that time, authority was respected, obedience revered and independent thinking discouraged. As a girl, Terry was taught "not to make waves". And yet, after watching all of these uncomplaining, bald, mutilated women dying painful heroic deaths, she decided that the price of obedience was just too high. In time, she came to believe that the fear and inability to question authority that killed rural Utah communities was the same fear that she saw in her mother's body; (and maybe in those blank pages). When she was arrested for protesting at the Mercury Nuclear Test site, a female officer frisking her body found a pen and pad of paper tucked into her boot. "What are these, she asked?" Their eyes met and Williams replied "weapons" and then smiled as she pulled the leg of her trouser back down over her boot.[74]

TRAUMA: TIME, SPACE and FRACTALS

In 1995 Terry Tempest Williams visited Hiroshima. From the old campus of the University of Hiroshima, just a few kilometers from the epicenter of the atomic bomb blast, she walked over to their Red Cross Hospital. This facility was the only semi-functioning hospital after the explosion. Building Six is dedicated to atomic bomb research and patient care. Sadako Sasaki died here on October 25, 1955, of leukemia. Dozens of vibrantly colored origami cranes hang from the ceiling, outside rooms and around the nurse's station. This cancer ward, up on the fourth floor, feels all too familiar to this American *hibakusha* who knows what lives and dies in these rooms. "It feels", Williams wrote, "as though the collective grief of Japan is hidden behind each closed door."

The author was invited by the University of Hiroshima Department of Literature, and The Japanese Association for the Study of Literature and the Environment, to give a reading. She introduced herself as a *hibakusha*, read from *The*

Clan of One Breasted Women and then spoke of her family's struggles with her mother's and other deaths and their relationship to nuclear testing. Blind obedience, she said, in the name of patriotism or religion ultimately takes our lives. At the end of her presentation she faced a terrifying silence… a stoic sea of *tatemae*; their cultural mandate against the disclosure of true feelings, *baka shojiki* (meaning foolishly honest, imprudent, naïve and immature). Looking down at her text, very softly she said that she was embarrassed to have told them her story, "I cannot imagine what you have endured together within your families, your communities. Please know the empathy I feel". Silence. Nothing. No response.

Now feeling desperate Williams asked for their thoughts. More silence. At last, an elderly professor replied, "You must understand it is very complicated for us. We are evading you." And then a woman in tears dared to speak. "We are still under an ethos of silence. Our misery continues but we remain quiet. We know that we are dependent on the United States for economic and political stability." A woman seated next to her continued; "Many *hibakusha* have told their stories and campaigned courageously for the elimination of nuclear weapons around the world, but many of them are now dead. Truth remains among the common citizenry but it is not spoken of." After a pause, she continued, "My grandmother said to me", "I do not want to speak of these things". Another then added, "It is an American's nature to resist. Our Japanese nature is to feel shame." [75]

We now live in a world where the plight of *hibakusha* and their descendants extends far beyond Utah, the American Southwest and Japan. Many remain unaware, and downwinders now number in the unknown millions throughout our entire Northern Hemisphere. We cannot forget that the USA conducted nuclear test explosions in the South Pacific, Alaska, Colorado, Mississippi and New Mexico. In addition there have been an estimated 2,000 nuclear tests conducted worldwide by Great Britain, France, China, the former USSR, India, Pakistan and North Korea. Israel is known to have a nuclear arsenal and probably Iran as well. Adding to this danger, we have had at least three known nuclear reactor disasters; at Three Mile Island, Chernobyl and now the Fukushima Daiichi complex. All of these events have infused vast quantities of radioactive material into our planetary biosphere, which has been widely dispersed and deposited as global fallout and malignant contamination. There are now 700 nuclear facilities on the planet with more under construction. Nevertheless, the myth of necessity and the fairy tale of "perfectly safe" nuclear energy remains largely unchallenged. Meanwhile radiation's known potential to cause lethal diseases, mutations and other genetic defects raises the probability that The Bomb and all of its iterations has now become an integral part of our human family.

TRAUMA: TIME, SPACE and FRACTALS

9

OUR HOUSE DIVIDED

"A house divided against itself, cannot stand"

(Abraham Lincoln, 1858)

...and soon now we shall go out of the house and go into the convulsion of the world, *out of history into history and the awful responsibility of time.*

(Robert Penn Warren, *All the King's Men*)

Historians, terrorists and media savvy politicians know that anniversary dates of events involving unresolved trauma can serve as temporal markers for whatever remains unfinished from the past. In the view of Southern novelist Shelby Foote, "If you look at American history as the lifespan of a man, the Civil War represents the great trauma of our adolescence. It's the sort of experience you never forget." This conflict which raged from 1861-1865, killed at least a half million men, maimed countless others, traumatized families and devastated a humiliated South for generations. Now, as we are in the midst of events commemorating the 150th anniversary of this American tragedy, echoes of our blood stained fratricidal conflict continue to reverberate throughout our politics and culture. Until today, there is still no agreement as to what this war was really about.[76]

By way of disclosure, I grew up in the Northeastern US where Calvinist roots still fed the public faith that our government had the ability to do good; and a middle class work ethic still prevails. More specifically, we lived just outside of New York City, modeled on its original namesake New Amsterdam. From the start, this area served as an international commercial trading society; multi-ethnic, multi-religious and materialistic, where no one ethnic or religious group has ever been truly in charge. This region has a profound tolerance for diversity, an unflinching commitment to freedom of inquiry and a great respect for intellectual achievement. [77]

TRAUMA: TIME, SPACE and FRACTALS

Most public schools taught that the American Civil War was fought to preserve the Union and free the slaves. While there was mention of the fact that factories and marketplaces of northern industrialists profited from commodities delivered by slave labor such as cotton, rice, indigo and tobacco, this was not the emphasis. While I am glad that the Northern forces won and our Union was preserved, I remain saddened by the excesses and atrocities visited upon our southern brethren who held distinctly different values.

The culture of the Deep South was founded and developed, in a large part, by Barbados slave lords and the region continued as a bastion of authoritarian white supremacy where democracy was the privilege of the few. Southern society was militarized, caste structured and deferential to authority. There remains a deeply rooted, faith based distrust of secular education. This area was also the well spring of African-American culture whose obedience to their Caucasian overlords was enforced by state sponsored racism.[78] As a schoolchild, my only exposure to a southern view of the war was of a beloved aunt taking me to see the epic production of *Gone With the Wind* (1939), with its picturesque plantation-lands of gentility, romantic Cavaliers and cotton fields; masters and slaves. Southern aristocrats, isolated from the realities of war, welcomed, glamorized and hoped for their rebellion against the North. Any who dared to disagree were branded as cowards or traitors. Mounted upon their magnificent steeds, Confederate soldiers rode off to war dressed in ribbons and silk sashes, after promising loved ones that they would soon return unharmed and victorious. [79]

I still remember being alternately enthralled and then horrified by an epic cinematic sweep through the Old South, the Civil War and the bitter aftermath of the Reconstruction Era. This three hour and forty-five minute version of Margaret Mitchell's Pulitzer Prize winning (1,037 page) novel, (first published in 1936), was made at a time when segregation was law in the South and reality in the North. After the Bible, this novel is still the most popular book in America and the film is considered to be something of a national treasure. *Gone with the Wind* has re-appeared in a series of revivals featuring a gauzy patina of antebellum luxury, soon followed by a broken and bleeding Confederacy. A number of these now classic scenes, and memorable dialogues, have become an integral part our national psyche. Many of us remember them now, exactly as they were penned, by a novelist's dream of a fantasized civilization ... gone with the wind.

In our region it was generally agreed that the Civil War was long over, and brave Northern Yankees had won a moral and political triumph. This aspect of our history was most certainly not a topic of daily conversation. In the South however, where this conflict is known as, "The War of Northern Aggression", regional and cultural perceptions are very different. Mark Twain's contention, that in the South "The war here is what "AD" is everywhere else; they date from it", may be an exaggeration, but not by much. The "scourge of the Damn Yankees" is still a daily topic which lives on in their collective folk memory. Un-reconciled Southerners maintain that the main thrust of the war was to establish Northern domination in commerce and culture. This also meant that Yankees intended to deny them their "way of life" which happened to include owning an inferior race of slaves. African Americans take a dim view of this self-serving revisionism. From their point of view, the South fought for the freedom to enslave their fellow men, women and children.

These vastly differing views recently surfaced with a sharply focused view of Charleston, South Carolina's December 19th, 2010 "Secession Ball". This fancy dress gala and other events were organized to celebrate the glory days of secession, when eleven states declared their sovereignty under a banner of state's rights and broke from the Union to form their rebel Confederacy. The Palmetto State was the first to secede declaring that, "All are united now with few exceptions in the belief that a stand must be made for African slavery or it's forever lost". Ninety percent of delegates attending this secession convention were slaveholders.[80]

Even so, this inconvenient subject of slavery was dismissed during an hour long anniversary play organized by the sponsoring Confederate Heritage Trust in order to re-enact this convention of December 19, 1860. "Secession delegates", their narrator concluded, "did not act for glory, riches, honor, or to preserve the institution of slavery, they acted for freedom alone". At their glittering evening gala (for the price of a $100 a ticket, an invitation promised a joyous night of food and drink) many of these 300, all white attendees, donned antebellum attire. As the liquor flowed, Cavalier planters and hoop skirted, corseted belles were inspired to join the chorus in a rousing rendition of the Confederate anthem; *Dixie* (a synonym for the Southern United States):

I wish I was in the Land of Cotton, Old times there are not forgotten...
Look away! Look away! Look away, Dixieland.

The overall mood of this "Look Away", rose-colored, denial-laced, costume gala was festive and defiant. One could almost be forgiven for thinking that the whole town of Charleston had travelled back in time. Outside of South Carolina's commemorative ball the mood was anything but festive and there was no mistaking the time as any other than the 21st century. More than a hundred, mostly black, protesters carried signs saying, "Don't celebrate Slavery and Terrorism" and, "It's **not** about Heritage". "*Slavery* is what you defend when you have a party, a celebration, get drunk, holler loud like a rebel, and talk about how you're celebrating your heritage", said National Association for the Advancement of Colored People leader Reverend Nelson B. Rivers III. "No matter how you dress it up, it is still *slavery*." I can only imagine what kind of celebration they would have if they won", added Lonnie Rudolph, President of the South Carolina NAACP.[81] As darkness fell, protesters lit candles and sang *We Shall Overcome*, an old gospel song from the Deep South that became an anthem of the African-American Civil Rights Movement (1955-1968). In writing about what she terms Post-Traumatic Slave Syndrome, Joy Degrury Leary, describes our former slave based economy as a kind of African-American Holocaust involving an estimated 20 to 30 million blacks, captured and sold into captivity.

The distance between these two realities underscores how divisive the topic of the Civil War has remained. These two sides can't even agree on something as basic as the names of battles. Southerners tended to name battles after nearby towns such as Manassas, which the North refers to as Bull Run.

TRAUMA: TIME, SPACE and FRACTALS

One could imagine, and in fact it was the hope of many, that the election of Barack Hussein Obama as the 44th President of the United States could go a long way toward the healing of this long standing national wound. In his inaugural address Mr. Obama acknowledged the change his election represented, describing himself as the son of an African father, who less than 60 years ago might not have been served in a restaurant. After taking the oath of office on the same Bible that was used by President Abraham Lincoln at his first inaugural in 1861, President Obama emphasized his determination to unite Americans in meeting the challenges facing our nation. Obama has often referred to Lincoln, the great emancipator and nemesis of the Confederate South, as an ongoing source of inspiration.

The ascension of a black man to the White House was indeed historic in light of the fact that back-breaking black slave labor was used in its construction; twelve of his presidential predecessors had held slaves and some brought them along as servants. Michelle Obama, our new First Lady has both white and Native American ancestors and is descended from South Carolina slaves. Mrs. Obama now has a staff of 26 attending to her needs. While Mr. Obama identifies himself as black, his mother was white. These mixed race people, and their children, taking up residence in the White House was received as an insult and a provocation by southern and other white supremacists.

Not surprisingly the Ku Klux Klan was swift to react. The Knights of the Ku Klux Klan, one of our nation's earlier terrorist organizations, was founded during the aftermath of the Civil War as a white supremacist insurgency of former Confederate rebels. Best known for vigilante violence, hooded, white sheeted hangmen, disguised as ghosts, cried out for societal purging. These racist zealots launched terrorizing night rides through dark forests, bull whips cracking; eager to gather in local pastures for ceremonial burning of their hate filled crosses of warning. [82] While in present time the media savvy face of the contemporary incarnation of the Klan has changed, their organized bigotry has not. As long as this mindset exists, it will find some means of expression.[83] This modern Klan has close ties with neo-Nazis and other radical right hate groups and they remain a political and societal force to be reckoned with. Membership in these groups has grown exponentially since the candidacy and election of Barack Obama and they maintain a bold presence on the internet.

Neo-Nazi, former Grand Wizard of the KKK, former Louisiana State Representative, and candidate in both Republican and Democratic presidential primaries, David Duke describes himself as a "nationalist" and "racial realist" who maintains that "all people have a basic human right to preserve their heritage". In response to Obama's meteoric rise in national politics, Duke rallied his supporters with an essay entitled, *"A Black Flag for White America"*:

"Obama is like that new big dark spot on your arm that finally sends you to the doctor for some real medicine....Obama is the pain that lets your body know that something is dreadfully wrong. Obama will let the American people know that there is a real cancer eating away at the heart of our country and Republican aspirin will not only not cure it, but masks the pain and makes you think that you don't need radical surgery." [84]

For white supremacists, especially in the South and Southwest, having a black man in the White House represents an insult to their honor. The relationship between cultures of honor and violence is a subject in itself which is here limited to its relevance to the history of our country. According to Psychology Professor Richard Nisbett, the South radiates a "culture of honor", where any affront or sign of violence is to be avenged. A key aspect of this culture is the importance of the insult and the necessity to respond to it. An insult implies that the target is weak enough to be bullied. Since a reputation for strength is the essence of a culture of

TRAUMA: TIME, SPACE and FRACTALS

honor, any individual who issues the insult must be forced to retract. If the instigator refuses he must be punished with violence or even death.[85] This is particularly important if an insult involves a woman. In Bill Bryson's memoir of the Fifties he cites this following example of "southern honor", avenging a lady in segregated Alabama:

Mobile: The Alabama Supreme Court yesterday upheld a death sentence imposed on a Negro handyman, Jimmy Wilson, 55, for robbing Mrs. Estelle Barker of $1.95 in her home last year. Mrs. Barker is white.

Although robbery is a capital offence in Alabama, no one has been executed in the state for theft of less than $5. A court official suggested that the jury had been influenced by the fact that Mrs. Barker told the jury that Wilson had spoken to her in a disrespectful manner.

A spokesman for the National Association for the Advancement of Colored People called the death sentence "a sad blot on the nation" but said the organization is unable to aid the condemned man because it is barred in Alabama.

The Des Moines Register, August 23, 1958 [86]

The Encyclopedia of Southern Culture is replete with accounts of feuds, duels, lynching, ambush and bushwhacking. The South evolved this way, Nisbett argues, because it was settled by a number of swashbuckling Cavaliers of noble and landed gentry who coveted "knightly medieval standards of manly honor and virtue". Next to arrive was a wave of Scottish and Irish immigrant herders. These newcomers were tribal, pastoral and warlike men who steadfastly upheld an ancient tradition that a man's reputation is central to his economic survival. During and after the Civil War many of these immigrant Celts spread out to settle the territories of the western frontier. Out there in the Old West, the culture of honor continued onward in a colorful guise of cowboy gunslingers, high noon shootouts, bullwhips, ambushes, and vigilante justice.[87] To this day, western regions maintain a strong attachment to all manner of firearms, deep distrust of the Federal Government and widespread suspicion that Obama is planning to take away their guns. Bumper stickers such as, "*You can have my gun, bullets first*", are fairly indicative of the regional mood. There are many similar messages out and around on our national highways, "*Gun *control is not about guns, it's about control*"; "*All those in favor of gun control raise both hands*"; "*Stick to your guns*"; and my personal favorite, "*You can have my gun when you pry it from my cold dead hands*". And yes, many of these people are willing to die rather than give up their guns. They don't trust any centralized authority and, "there might be another civil war."

Lincoln's "house divided" analogy was perfect for our country in a time of crisis. Our sixteenth president offered an image that evokes the psychic architecture of a nation as a collection of rooms under one roof. Yet, his profound commitment to an authentic, family-like, post-war reconciliation was not continued by his successors. If the United States of America is a family, it has come to resemble one that has resolved to never speak with much openness or honesty about the terrible things that have transpired within our divided house. On a recent trip through the South where Civil War culture was presented as "authentic", journalist

TRAUMA: TIME, SPACE and FRACTALS

Peter Birkenhead observed that it was indeed all very interesting, but not authentic. While their okra was outstanding, black-eyed peas delicious, and hospitality gracious, he couldn't help noticing that they just left out "the slavery part". Upon reflection, he asks, "what is willful forgetting of slavery if not the cover-up of a crime, an abdication of its victims and of ourselves?" In unresolved trauma, the past is always with us. The path toward historical resolution entails a cultural necessity to acknowledge and integrate the good, the bad and the mythic, if we are to be fully present with our current crises.[88]

10

THE TREE OF LIBERTY

"We have the purpose of preventing bigots and ignoramuses from controlling the United States"

(Clarence Darrow, Scopes Monkey Trial, 1925)

..."*we're in a tailspin. The need for voices of reason, simple and eloquent, has never been stronger.*

(Bill Moyers, January, 2012)

This fear of a black president " who wants to take away our guns and our freedom", has been an enormous boon to the so called Tea Party movement founded shortly after Barack Obama's inauguration in January, 2009. These right wing zealots claim that their ultra-patriotic cause harks back to our Revolutionary War when the original Thirteen Colonies were rebelling against the oppressive policies of the British Empire. During a violent insurrection on December 16, 1773, as part of an increasing rebellion against unfair taxation, colonists dumped bails of English tea into Boston Harbor. This iconic event in American history came to be known as The Boston Tea Party.[89] While staging public protests and media grandstanding, latter day tea partyers are proud to brandish a mix of historic and modern weapons. If any doubt remains as to the aggressive nature of these gatherings, the message is on their Revolutionary War era flag, which features a coiled rattlesnake ready to strike. A venomous serpent appears against a bright yellow field along with words of warning, "Don't Tread on Me".

Many of these protesters are fond of parading around in Revolutionary War era costumes and other patriotic get-ups defiantly festooned with commercial teabags. One of their most popular and provocative placards reads, "Time to Water the Tree of Liberty". Here they refer to the statement made by Founding Father, Thomas Jefferson (1743-1826): "The Tree of Liberty must be refreshed from time to time with the blood of patriots and tyrants". This message, now popular with a wide range of extremists, has been widely replicated on tee shirts, bumper stickers, internet web sites, forums and chat rooms. Here I wish to note that Thomas Jefferson, principal author of The Declaration of Independence, and third President of the United States had six unacknowledged children with a black slave woman named Sally Hemmings, one of the 150 he owned at his Monticello Plantation.

Cloaked in a mantle of state's rights, these bellicose tea bagging patriots want to "take our country back" (to all white Christian control). Like their Puritan forbearers, these minions of the far Right tend to see their world as defined by a conflict between forces of light and darkness. According to them, the "forces of good" are decent, conservative, conformist; "real" Americans, mostly white, married, fundamentalist Christians. These self-righteous souls see themselves as standing in a Holy War of fierce opposition to a wide variety of diabolical figures: liberals, gays, lesbians, trans-genders, Muslims, Mexicans, socialists and other "foreigners". For these sanctimonious patriots, this first black president is a dangerous foreigner and illegitimate occupant of the Oval Office.[90] Citing the constitutional requirement that our Chief Executives are required to be American born, the Tea Party persists in the belief that Obama is really an African, born in Kenya. Furthermore, his Hawaiian birth certificate is alleged to be a fake, and therefore his presidency is illegal. All the while they deny that these allegations have anything to do with race. These same Tea Party patriots had no qualms about voting for John McCain; Obama's white Republican opponent, who was born in Panama.

This increasingly divisive movement has been actively encouraged by our opportunistic media who are quick to seize an opportunity to cover any national or international political circus. The colorful antics of the Tea Party rarely disappoint and members will shout themselves hoarse for the benefit of nearly any video camera. All of our major media outlets have afforded reactionary Tea Party spokespersons more than ample opportunity to trumpet their mean spirited rumors that President Obama's parents were not married. And then these "patriots" are encouraged to rave on and on with their lunatic accusations that our president is a secret Muslim terrorist, with a secret Hitler mustache, socialist, space alien, and tyrant who plans to enslave white people, especially women as sex slaves to black men. A Kansas Tea Party, anti-Obama web site featured an image of the president as a skunk, "half-black, half-white and everything it does stinks".[91] Many of the faith based loyalists are also convinced that this black impostor is also the Anti-Christ who is destined to bring about the inevitable Armageddon. The Tea Party's rabid religious right went so far as to accuse Michelle Obama and her mother of practicing witchcraft in the White House.

While I could go on about the ideological excesses of our corporate controlled, Christo-fascist Tea Party fringe, this is not the purpose of this chapter. More important is a concern that millions have been bamboozled by their bold-faced lies and fear mongering theatrics. One is tempted to laugh away the blatant nonsense spewing forth from this coalition of dunces. Nevertheless, serious attention is warranted since Tea Party candidates, funded by conservative corporate elites, have done very well in local and national elections. Now, one is left to wonder how much the widespread fear of immigrants, blacks, and other people of color and culture has to do with their recent electoral successes.

The right to bear arms is an essential part of any Tea Party candidate's rhetoric and this carries an inherent threat of violence, if they don't get their way. This was spelled out in clear language in the recent campaign of Republican Sharon Angle in Nevada. The perpetually smiling candidate warned that if her party did not prevail at the ballot box, they might need to resort to "Second Amendment Remedies", (guns) and "take her opponent out" (assassination). Mercifully, Angle lost that election, but only by a narrow margin. Most of the prominent Tea Party candidates enjoy brandishing their personal firearms as part of their video sound-bites and campaign promotional literature.

Now, in Autumn of 2011, a much greater and more inclusive rebellion is taking over our national story. Three decades dominated by the regressive Right has finally provoked a progressive backlash. This new reality tells us what time it is in America. The 2008 hope for change has now become a demand. The vast majority of those who voted for President Obama as a longed for agent of change, have now realized that change will not come down from above. Millions who have given up on this president now turn to each other for solutions. We now have a situation whereby both those who fear Obama and those who feel betrayed by his campaign promises are ready for something new. And so, increasingly inflammatory populist rhetoric is rapidly moving past talk of firearms toward an invocation of the guillotine. American citizens have become accustomed to lingering tensions between North and South, and threats of guns and gun control, but these recent calls for the guillotine evoke a very different dynamic. During the French Revolution, their National Razor became a symbol for violent revolution when masses overthrew and executed many of their leaders. Perhaps you will remember that this revolutionary bloodbath began as a food riot. When starving peasants marched to Versailles to complain to their monarch that they had no more bread, they were met with a royal response which sounded something like, "Let them eat cake".

TRAUMA: TIME, SPACE and FRACTALS

While it is likely that such an insensitive statement, attributed to Queen Marie Antoinette, is not historically accurate, this iconic message has persisted as a warning to any privileged few who ignore the needs of the many.

Here in our already divided country, a new fault line of dissent broke out on September 17, 2011 with the Occupy Wall Street Protests against America's financial sector as a symbolic target of populist discontent. For the OCW protesters the roots of the Tree of Liberty have been poisoned by government sanctioned corporate greed. Crime and government policy have become indistinguishable. Millions have woken up to the reality of a soaring income gap, public services cut, illegal foreclosures, neighborhoods wrecked, massive debt and tuition hikes. Something finally clicked in this country which prides itself on promoting an egalitarian society. Initially ignored by corporate controlled mainstream media, the smoldering embers and sparks of uprising soon flew off and spread like wild fire to over 100 American cities.

Soon thereafter small towns and rural communities took up the cause. In tiny Moser, Oregon (population 430), as described on www.occupywallstreet.com, they have no traffic lights, and a single gas station that closed years ago. Working together with participants from other small communities of the Columbia Gorge, they have established the nation's smallest Occupy camp. This self-organizing collective plans to reach out to those who don't agree with them. Often they find that after ten minutes of conversation they discover that most of them have more upon which to agree than disagree. Occupy by the Gorge is setting up 15 or more tents to attract visitors and even invited local Tea Party activists to come over and share tea and round-table discussions about areas where the Tea Party and Occupy movements can agree.

TRAUMA: TIME, SPACE and FRACTALS

Protesters are now coming from *all* regions, *all* walks of life and a widening political spectrum. They take to the streets, parks and barricades to represent their 99 percent of the population excluded from the concentrations of wealth and political power controlled by the richest one percent of "economic royalists". Their family incomes are declining while the incomes of the rich and super-rich, especially those in finance, continue to soar. Moreover, the rich pay less taxes on their astronomical profits, often derived from the subsidized outsourcing of jobs to cheap labor in Third World countries. Too much money in the hands of too few sets up a volatile climate in times of catastrophic levels of unemployment, crushed unions, unaffordable health care, demolished regulation, unpopular wars , decline in services, intrusive surveillance, erosion of civil liberties and a growing resentment of Wall Street's control of both political parties. Support is growing for "The Second American Revolution". Scattered throughout these crowds one hears cries of "off with their heads". On October 4th, 2011, *People Like Us* web site carried an article entitled "Wall Street – Off With Their Heads" (www.peoplelikeus.com/?=17190) featuring an engraving of a guillotine in use for public executions.

Online readers were referred to a recent RT (Russian Television) interview with comedienne Roseanne Bar who says that she favors a return of the guillotine. She began by challenging the absurd legal fiction that "corporations are people". According to Roseanne, if corporations and big banks are "people" as the Supreme Court recently ruled, then they should all be tried for murder, fraud, larceny, mayhem and then summarily beheaded. Here one hopes that Roseanne exaggerated in order to make a point, and still her choice of words evokes a disturbing historical precedent. Predictive market analyst and financial expert Max Keiser, who is not a comedian, followed up her message on October

10, 2011. During the televised *Max Keiser Report* he warned that "the mob is beginning to circle". His message to the One Percent: "We've got the guillotine". This advice was soon followed by Trends Research Institute's founder, Gerald Celente. In his October 15th, 2011, "Let them eat cake" interview with Alex Jones on InfoWars.com, Celente opined that the elites now had "an image at the back of their heads of the guillotine that would soon be playing in a theater near them".

Any mention of the guillotine, even in jest, invokes a host of disturbing images. This along with the right wing, corporate bankrolled, Tea Partyer's call for "blood of martyrs" and " second amendment remedies" (firearms) is the language of murderous rage and does not bode well for our immediate future. While most of the factions may look back to the mythical unity of our Founding Fathers with notions of "Freedom" and "Liberty", there is no agreement as to how these concepts should be translated into contemporary American life.

Those who study history understand that any extreme is destined to become its opposite. This dynamic has many names. In the Ancient World, Greeks described this as a principle of *enantiodromia,* whereby that which is extreme has a tendency to morph into its opposite. Other versions of this principle advise that you are likely to "become what you resist" or "what you resist, persists" and "you become what you hate". Swiss psychiatrist C.G. Jung held that a superabundance of any force will eventually produce its opposite. This, he believed to be the equivalent to the principle of equilibrium in the natural world. Any extreme, therefore, will be opposed because of a systemic need to restore balance. At this point, it seems somewhat early to be able to forecast the outcome for our nation-wide protests which are likely to become part of something global. What appears to have the makings of an all-out class war may actually be the stirring of something greater. As activist author Naomi Wolf observed, "We may be witnessing the first large global conflict where people are aligned by consciousness and not nation or religion".[92] Nevertheless, we can be sure that extremes on any side will, soon or later, evolve into their opposite and these cycles of conflict will continue.

TRAUMA: TIME, SPACE and FRACTALS

11

OLD MYTHS AND REMEMBERED GLORIES

"Southerners are very strange about that war"

(Shelby Foote, The Civil War: A Narrative)

*Somethings happening here.
What it is ain't exactly clear...*

(Buffalo Springfield song: "For What it's Worth")

It could be argued that our country has now become so dangerously polarized that we must prepare to face a possibility of another civil war. This new reality includes recent threats of secession and a possible breakup of our over-extended global empire, which was once known as a democratic republic. As a child, I remember being taught to "Pledge allegiance to the flag and to the republic for which it stands". How many who recite this oath of allegiance realize that our republic no longer exists. Our democracy has long since evolved into a global empire. Even more challenging is the current reality that we are now an empire in decline and our Union is again in danger of disintegration. History has shown that empires rarely learn in time because power tends to dull people's capacity for self-reflection. While declining in power, imperial regimes desperately cling to old myths and remembered glory.[93] Former White House Press Secretary to President Lyndon B. Johnson, and public commentator Bill Moyers recently acknowledged this reality. Despite our global ambitions, Moyers believes that we remain a nation divided. He offered the following insight during an interview with *History News Network*, on August 24, 2011:

And suddenly we're back in the mindset of the 1850's when politics couldn't serve any of the great issues dividing the country, above all slavery. Like the radical Right today, there were large numbers of people who wanted nothing to do with the Federal Government and wanted the Federal Government to do nothing, and also there were large numbers of people who wanted the Federal Government to carry out policies in the interest of all citizens. It took a bloody Civil War to settle what politics couldn't.

It has become increasingly clear that White Supremacists, radical Religious Right Wingers and Tea Party extremists, consider President Obama to be our major problem and the cause of our nation's decline. From a systemic perspective, however, it is more likely that the virulent nature of their resistance to this historic presidency is a symptom of a much deeper problem. This resistance cannot be about politics since Obama's administration has scrupulously followed nearly all the socially repressive policies of the previous Republican, conservative, war mongering, Bush/Cheney regime. The real problem is that the festering wounds of our Civil War have not yet healed. The presence of a black man in the White House, serving as our Chief Executive and American representative on the world stage, has brought this to light. And, it could be that the threat of another civil war needs to be taken seriously in light of the culture war now underway.

President Obama will likely stand for re-election as the Democratic candidate in 2012 and it is likely that the faith based Tea Party will have a major role in choosing his Republican opponent. Texas Governor Rick Perry, an Evangelical, Tea Party favorite and current front runner, once named confederate General Robert E. Lee as one of the historical personages that he would most like to have dinner with. Perry has roots in the Confederate cause. His great-great grandfather was an ex-confederate who re-settled in Texas. Governor Perry grew up during segregation and the family's private hunting preserve was called "Niggerhead". A recent article in *Alter-Net* asks, "Would a Perry versus Obama Contest be a Confederacy versus Union Rematch?" Journalist Adele Stan argues that if Perry should win the Republican nomination, an obvious sub-text would be Confederacy versus the Union, a theme reinforced by each candidate's race.

While this Lone Star candidate will likely prove too provincial to gain the nomination, the fact that he attained front-runner status is telling. In 2009, one of Perry's speeches was interrupted by cries, "Secede!" When the governor was asked to respond to reports associating him with the idea of state sovereignty and secession, he replied that... "Texas is a unique place. When we came into the Union in 1845, one of the issues was that we would be able to leave if we decided to do that." [94]

For neo-Confederate hopefuls, a Perry victory would signal that their "lost cause" would rise again from the ashes of their short-lived, fallen and failed nation. This notion was woven into southern culture following the publication of a novel: *The Lost Cause: A New Southern History of the War of the Confederates,* by Edward Pollard, a Virginia journalist, just a year after the war ended. In what has been described as a "gold rush of nostalgic forgetting" the novel unfolds as a "breathless, self-pitying fantasy, and the first of many to recast the conflict as a tragedy of fraternal strife and regional repression". The defeat of the Confederacy is attributed to the overwhelmingly superior resources and underhanded tactics of the North. The South's most ruthless generals are exalted as paragons of honor, while freed people run amok, and families hold tearful post-war reunions to mourn the loss of their antebellum idyll of hoop skirts and happy-go-lucky chattel. Slavery is depicted as a benign and beneficial institution. These and other works to follow, helped to construct a southern culture of perpetual grievance, wounded pride, and revisionist stories of an imagined past.[95]

This nostalgic theme of "the lost cause" is a prominent feature in the history of Civil War re-enactments along with a belief that "a cause remembered is not really lost". Re-enacting began even before the war was over as a way for soldiers to remember fallen comrades, and to show family, friends and onlookers, what events in camp, drills and battle looked like. Modern re-enactments began to gain popularity during the Civil War Centennial commemorations of 1961-1965 in the midst of the highly contentious Civil Rights Movement. Despite some apparent good intentions, many commemorative events devolved into embarrassing disasters. There was no denying that in the one hundred years since these battles, presumably fought to grant full civil rights to African Americans, blacks were still fighting to ensure those rights. For government friendly media outlets, it became increasingly difficult to attempt to either ignore or present any balanced coverage of our nation's conflicted reality. With historical hindsight, the situation was quite clear; American citizens of color were being vehemently opposed by state's rights segregationists who resurrected their Confederate "stars and bars" battle flag as a symbol of white supremacy. This defiant red flag; a diagonal blue cross studded with white stars on a blazing field of crimson, further inflamed emotions on both sides of the Civil Rights conflict dating back to the Civil War era.[96] When the war ended there was no truth and re-conciliation commission to come together to process memories; no Nuremberg trials to promote reflection and no Great Emancipator to free the future from the past. The emotional and spiritual needs of national re-conciliation were quickly subverted in the interest of political expediency on both sides of the Mason Dixon line.[97]

Robert J. Cook wrote a history of the centennial that should give our nation pause as we stumble toward this sesquicentennial: "If that Civil War centennial tells us anything, it is that seemingly entrenched historical memories are not always a match for the onrush of time." For African-Americans, emancipation was in fact followed by at least another hundred years of state sponsored subjugation, Black Codes, Jim Crow laws, peonage, convict leasing, domestic terrorism and lynching. As blacks and other minorities continue to struggle for equality, the romance of the lost cause continues to dominate widespread conceptions of what the Civil War means for us today.[98] Images of a bow-and-curtsy era of moonlight and magnolias still pervade revisionist memories of a bloody awful, tragic conflict that should repel and horrify any sensible patriot.

WARGASM

Now that sesquicentennial commemorative events are underway we have an opportunity to take a deeper look into the practice of Civil War re-enactment and some of the many enthusiasts involved in these activities. From a trauma perspective, we know that unresolved traumas tend to repeat and even be re-enacted in one form or another which can be replicated down through the generations. A systemic view of this phenomenon holds that family patterns re-iterate and that anniversary dates and history of place often have a role in these repetitions. Members of a system who have met a difficult fate, which may also involve a perpetrator-victim dynamic, can pass their unresolved issues along to others and to their descendants in the form of "entanglements". Others in the system can then form hidden, unconscious or even conscious bonds with these unfortunate others. The epigenetic documentary, *The Ghost in Your Genes,* puts forth persuasive evidence that ancestral and collective memories from the past can be chemically imprinted within our genome. The question then arises, how to understand and relate to these memories which may or may not be traumatic or the result of entanglements.

There was a time when many trauma specialists believed that it was healing to relive detailed memories of traumatic events, and this has turned out to be largely untrue. Many past life therapists would not agree, but that is another subject. Nevertheless, it is true that many traumatized people feel a need to revisit unresolved events in one form or another. One of these forms is a compulsive urge or a strong pull toward re-enactment. In *Confederates in the Attic: Dispatches*

TRAUMA: TIME, SPACE and FRACTALS

from the Unfinished Civil War, Pulitzer Prize winning journalist Tony Horwitz, takes a thoughtful, entertaining, and often bittersweet look at hard core Civil War re-enacters. As a fellow Civil War enthusiast and self-described "Civil War Bore", he begins his quest by placing himself under the tutelage of one Robert Lee Hodge. Often hired for Civil War movies, Hodge is described as a figure who looks as though he might have stepped out of a 19th century tintype; tall, rail thin, long pointed beard and butternut uniform so frayed and filthy that it hung like rags on a scarecrow. Hodge has mastered the art of the bloat where he clutches his stomach, falls to the ground, his belly swells, hands curl, cheeks puff out as his mouth contorts in rictus pain and astonishment like so many images of a battlefield corpse. "A real ice–breaker at parties", Hodge explained to the astonished Horwitz. [99]

Hodge is a revered member of a group of hardcore, authentic or "Progressive", re-enactors who strive to achieve an immersive experience of the same poor conditions suffered by the original soldiers; camping without tents and sleeping exposed to rain and cold. Freezing temperatures are endured from insufficient clothing and blankets. Progressives sleep campaign-style by spooning with each other for warmth in trenches formerly occupied by the dead. In summer, zealots are eager to endure blazing sun, dripping skies, mud and mosquitos. Subsisting on poor and insufficient seasonal rations they practice a steady regimen of work, marching and drill in worn and ill-fitting footwear. Participants are expected to starve themselves into the gaunt appearance of their famished historical counterparts. Hodge feels that he was more or less born into his role. His father, from Alabama with a vague allegiance to the Confederacy, named him after rebel commander Robert E Lee. For Hodge and his legion of followers, the goal of their immersions is to use suffering and deprivation to attain a "period rush" or time-travel high that he calls a "wargasm". These hard won highs, he readily admits, can become increasingly addictive. [100]

To this outside observer, who happens to be a traumatologist, one could speculate that these extreme immersions might qualify as a form of systemically entangled traumatic reenactment, where one feels compelled to enter into a past where he or she does not belong. The more someone re-enacts, there may arrive an increasing need to do it even more, or in an even more self-depriving, authentic way. As a result, increasingly obsessive behavior could generate a closed loop of endless repetition which is actually trying to resolve traumas belonging to a previous generation.

There are other categories of re-enactors which are somewhat less extreme. The so-called Farbs or "polyester soldiers" are those who spend little time and money maintaining authenticity with regard to uniforms, accessories, period language and behavior. The most common group of re-enactors are known as Mainstream and they lie somewhere between Progressives and Farbs. A typical Civil War Re-enactment takes place over a weekend where re-enactors arrive on Friday and spectators view simulated battles on Saturday and Sunday. Women and children often take part in these events as costumed civilians, and a few women also participate as female soldiers who engaged in combat disguised as men.

It is interesting to learn that most re-enactors come from states that had belonged to the Confederacy. Not surprisingly, there is a notable lack of African-Americans willing to portray those legions of slaves who were an essential part of the original drama. It's quite telling that not only do African-Americans usually not participate, they rarely even attend re-enactments.[101] Still, the fact remains that thousands of slaves bore arms for the Confederacy. The motives of these black soldiers were complex, to say the least. Some were promised freedom while others were ordered into battle at gunpoint. There were also slaves loyal to their masters who were more fearful of an unknown enemy from the North than a known oppressor from the South. Given these layers of complexity, it is not surprising that National Park Rangers report that Black people rarely visit Civil War battlefields.[102] This population is understandably unwilling to support these three dimensional hobbyists engaged in costume pageants that suggest the war was all about battles. Blacks reject these theatricals which hold that each side fought with equal courage and high moral purpose, in a war which had little or nothing to do with slavery. They know that this conflict didn't end in April of 1865 with a few handshakes and mutual appreciation of a war well fought. In reality, emancipation, the Civil War's most important outcome, produced a terrible and violent reckoning with the legacy of slavery that persisted on into the 20th century.

While it seems possible that many hard core Progressives are to some degree entangled with previous generations of war traumatized family members, what are we to make of the fact that there are now over 30,000 well-meaning re-enactors planning to participate in the sesquicentennial events? One can easily imagine that these faux battles between Billy Yank and Johnny Reb provide the illusion of participating in "living history" or becoming a part of something much larger than oneself. However, I seriously doubt that these scripted pageants have much to do with the much needed healing of a still festering national wound. Civil War historian Glenn Lafantasie finds any notion of re-enacting this national tragedy nothing less than perverse. All in all, he suggests that the best way to commemorate our Civil War is to do so by leaving this war to the dead rather than the living. Dressing up and impersonating soldiers in period costume for a weekend of play-acting hellish battles, over and over again, does not help the dead to find a peaceful rest. In general, academic historians tend to reject re-enacting because it is not history.[103]

TRAUMA: TIME, SPACE and FRACTALS

Many cultures believe that certain places hold something like "fields of memory" and many of these places have been the sites of dark and tragic events. It is not unusual, for those who visit Civil War battlefields, slave quarters, auction blocks, prisoner of war camps, and massacre sites, to experience a sense of heaviness and overall pall. It is a fact that there remain colorful legends of hauntings in and around Civil War era locations. Many visitors report apparitions of restless spirits who died sudden, violent deaths and now seem lost and wandering somewhere between the land of the living and the dead. If this is true, then these recreational re-enactments are likely to disturb these tormented souls as well as the spirit of place.

Professor Lafantasie suggests that there are ways to honor the dead; commemorate, and learn about history without indulging in phony re-enactments and genteel, hoop-skirted, whites only, balls.[104] One can begin by reading the 272 words of Lincoln's Gettysburg Address in which he spells out

TRAUMA: TIME, SPACE and FRACTALS

the entire meaning of the Civil War for the American people of his time and ours. His speech was delivered upon the dedication of the Soldiers National Cemetery at Gettysburg, Pennsylvania, on November 19, 1863.

> Four score and seven years ago, our fathers brought forth upon this continent a new nation: conceived in liberty, and dedicated to the proposition that all men are created equal.
>
> Now we are engaged in a great civil war. . .testing whether that nation, or any nation so conceived and so dedicated. . . can long endure. We are met on a great battlefield of that war.
>
> We have come to dedicate a portion of that field as a final resting place for those who here gave their lives that that nation might live. It is altogether fitting and proper that we should do this.
>
> But, in a larger sense, we cannot dedicate. . .we cannot consecrate. . . we cannot hallow this ground. The brave men, living and dead, who struggled here have consecrated it, far above our poor power to add or detract. The world will little note, nor long remember, what we say here, but it can never forget what they did here. It is for us the living, rather, to be dedicated here to the unfinished work which they who fought here have thus far so nobly advanced.

TRAUMA: TIME, SPACE and FRACTALS

> It is rather for us to be here dedicated to the great task remaining before us. . .that from these honored dead we take increased devotion to that cause for which they gave the last full measure of devotion. . . that we here highly resolve that these dead shall not have died in vain. . . that this nation, under God, shall have a new birth of freedom. . . and that government of the people. . .by the people. . .for the people. . . shall not perish from the earth.

Lincoln held forth the promise that this war would not be fought in vain. He envisioned a unified America emerging out of the old; a country more dedicated to its most cherished ideals, born out of the fire and ashes of war. His words elevated the significance of our Civil War beyond a fight simply to restore the Union. Confronting the nightmare realities of battle and war, he honored the Union men buried there, who gave their lives for the sake of their country. The president encouraged Americans then and now to focus on the warrior's sacrifice rather than on the reality of the soldier's suffering. Lincoln's words articulated the deeper meaning of the war which was to initiate a new era of equality and freedom.

Now as the sesquicentennial events are underway it seems clear that this new era of freedom and equality has yet to come about. Long standing divisions continue to widen. Here in 2011 we find ourselves in a politically polarized, social, racial, and economic stalemate. Once again, our nation's political tides are flowing in opposite directions. In one direction, military, industrial and corporate sponsored currents are flowing toward imperial Washington. Our Federal Government has come to represent the ambitions of an overreaching, war mongering, failing empire; increasing surveillance, repression and loss of civil liberties. In the opposite direction, populist tides reflect a determined backlash against increasing instances of government intrusion into every aspect of American life. A neo-secessionist movement is already underway as an assertion of both state's rights and individual liberties. Time will tell if our beleaguered country can reach a viable solution through democratic process. It could be that we are in for a modern version of The Fourth Reich, another Civil War, a second American Revolution or something quite different, as yet unforeseen.

TRAUMA: TIME, SPACE and FRACTALS

CONCLUSION

Time past and
Time future
What might have been and what has been
Points to one end
Which is always present.

T.S. Eliot (Burnt Norton: Four Quartets)

Now in the 21st century, as we approach the end of a Mayan long count, one could imagine that their calendar encoded both the fractal nature, of the Universe and of time itself. It has also been suggested that these ancient Time Keepers sought to understand and map the temporal flow of creation. Mayan cosmology included a past which always returned; on a new level, in the form of historical symmetries and cycles whose underlying patterns continue to unfold throughout the fabric of time. This is a world view that presents both challenges and opportunities. In the realm of social trauma we have seen some of these replicating patterns in events as diverse as Katyn, Fukushima and the Sesquicentennial of the American Civil War. There are many other patterns there for those who care to look. Important clues are evident in apparent coincidences and synchronicities. History of place is often relevant, as well as anniversary dates, especially those involving some form of separation or broken connection, which often trigger re-enactment phenomena.

While this remains an open ended inquiry, at this point it seems clear that self-replicating patterns in many forms of trauma are generated by a number of factors. Often one finds that something which needs to be acknowledged is covered up, lied about or denied. This was especially evident in the events surrounding Katyn, where apparent coincidence, connections and consequences appear throughout individual, family and collective experiences. Numerous clues to unsolved mysteries involve many factors within these alleged coincidences;

including specific dates, places and the identity of the victims.

In such cases the axiom "truth will out" applies to this ongoing nightmare and lack of accountability; as well as the will to revenge which has generated ongoing cycles of violence. Absence of accountability is also a factor in many patterns which are perpetuated when something, or many things, remain interrupted or otherwise unfinished.

In the case of the American Civil War it seems that much remains unfinished. For many Southerners, that "War of Northern Aggression" never really ended and we are just having a rather long "intermission".

It is the nature of systems to seek balance. This can mean that a state of imbalance will generate repetition in an ongoing search for resolution. Imbalances can be generated by nations engaged in the roles of perpetrator and victim, as is currently evident in the complex nuclear trauma bond involving the USA and Japan, as well as many other individuals and families caught up in nuclear events.

Within the realm of trauma, the past is always present. Now in present time, we are inundated with the unfinished business of previous events and this hinders us from imagining any future which could be totally different from our past. Therefore, a seemingly straightforward question such as "What time is it?" can lead us into a virtual hall of mirrors. Politicians and others who seek to exploit the collective are well aware of this as a tool for manipulation and power. Here in the USA any dictator that our leaders want to eliminate, in order to confiscate his country's resources, is identified as "another Hitler". The populace will then agree to war or assassination because, "Hitler wasn't stopped until it was too late". While *now* is not *then*, in the realm of trauma this is never clear. Therefore, re-enactment patterns continue in various other times and places with a similar underlying and unresolved dynamic.

So, is it now possible to foresee a future that is completely different from the past? This question assumes a solid, fixed body of time known as "the past"...which does not and never has existed. Closer to the truth is the fact that any attempt to understand what has come before, must include a kaleidoscopic view of a fluid reality which keeps changing; along with ever-shifting perceptions necessarily colored by the relative values of a specific time, place and culture. As George Orwell warned in *1984*, 'Who controls the past, controls the future: who controls the present controls the past." Here I would suggest that in our time, there still remains an element of choice as to how we choose to hold those perceptions within an area of consciousness that exists beyond the dictates of tribe, politics or religion. Recognition of the power of individual and collective choice is a key element in any and all attempts to resolve trauma.

TRAUMA: TIME, SPACE and FRACTALS

As we look toward 2012 and beyond, questions about our future have come to occupy the collective mind. Economist and Trends Researcher Gerald Celente, often lauded for his common sense assessment of reality, maintains that "current events predict future trends". While I admire Mr. Celente's succinct pragmatism, I rather prefer Bert Hellinger's spacious elaboration on this same perspective.

What time is it? It is time for that which has announced itself and is here already. ..The future announces itself within the present. It draws something to itself. Through its gravity, it sets something into motion before the future itself shows clearly. It is already affecting the present, making itself felt even while it is still hidden. It is only in our perception that the future lies somewhere in the distance. In reality, it is already here.

The future is in a space beyond time. How then do we deal with our future? We relate to it as if it were already here. So in our imagination we put time aside. We allow this future to unfold its power, even now. As an idea, as a source of power, the future is here already and just needs to manifest. (*Together in the Shadow of God*)

TRAUMA: TIME, SPACE and FRACTALS

If this is true, we are faced with the prospect of a future which is already here, and a past which keeps changing along with the perceptions of a previously agreed upon reality. Within this perspective, we find an immediate challenge: never lose sight of the power of choice for how we are to hold these ephemeral manifestations of what we understand as now.

APPENDIX

ATOMIC TESTS IN NEVADA

Thirty thousand copies of this small green pamphlet were issued in 1957 by the Atomic Energy Commission in order to convince local residents that the test site bomb blasts were benign. In *Atomic Soldiers; American Victims of Nuclear Experiments*, Howard L. Rosenberg suggests that this document belongs in the annals of social psychology as a hallmark in government attempts to propagandize the populace. This classic study in inaccurate and deliberate disinformation addresses the populace with the following claims:

You people who live near the Nevada test site are in a very real sense, active participants in the nation's atomic test program. You have been observers of tests which have contributed greatly to building the defenses of our country and of the Free World. ... Nevada tests have helped us to make great progress in a few years,

TRAUMA: TIME, SPACE and FRACTALS

and have been a vital factor in maintaining the peace of the world........Every test detonation in Nevada is carefully evaluated as to your safety before it is included in a schedule...Every phase of the operation is likewise studied from the safety viewpoint... Although some residents have been inconvenienced by the operations, to our knowledge no one outside the test site has been hurt in six years of testing....experience has proved the adequacy of the safeguards which govern the Nevada operations.

Simply stated, all such findings have confirmed that Nevada test fallout has not caused illness or injured the health of anyone living near the test site...many persons in Nevada, Utah, Arizona and California have Geiger counters. We can expect many reports that Geiger counters are going crazy today. Reports like this may worry people unnecessarily. Don't let them bother you. A Geiger counter can go completely off-scale in fallout which is far from hazardous.

This green pamphlet was illustrated with a cartoon drawing of an unshaven, bowlegged cowboy raising his eyebrows at a rapidly clicking Geiger counter.

TRAUMA: TIME, SPACE and FRACTALS

Notes:

---

[1] Lungold, Ian Xel (February 17, 2004) *Welcome to the Evolution: Solving the Mystery of the Mayan Calendar:* UFO TV DVD, White Horse, Canada.

[2] Richards, E.G. (March 2000) *Mapping Time: The Calendar and Its History.*

[3] Jenkins, John Major (2009) *The 2012 Story: The Myths, Fallacies and Truth Behind the Most Intriguing Dates in History,* pp. 13-16.

[4] Calleman, Carl Johan (August 19, 2009) " The Tortuguero Monument 6 and the Mayan End Date"
www.calleman.com/content/articles/the_tortuguero%20_monument.htm

[5] _____, (2004) *The Mayan Calendar and the Transformation of Consciousness,* pp.12-16.

[6] Jenkins, *op.cit.* pp. 137-148.

[7] Pinchbeck, Daniel (2010) *The Return of Quetzalcoatl,* p.224.

[8] Schele, Linda and David Freidel (1990) *A Forest of Kings : The Untold Story of the Ancient Maya*, p46. See also: Von Hagen, Victor Wolfgang (1900) *Mayan Explorer: John Lloyd Stephens and the Lost Cities of Central America and Yucatan.*

[9] Von Hagen, *op.cit,* p.198.

[10] Grossinger, Richard (2010) *2013: Raising the Earth to the Next Vibration,* pp.11-15 See also: Arguelles, Jose (2002) *Time and the Technosphere: The Law of Time and Human Affairs.*

[11] Selbe , Joseph and David Steinmetz (2001) *The Yugas: Keys to Understanding Our Hidden Past and Future Enlightenment,* offers an in-depth exploration of this complex and controversial topic.

TRAUMA: TIME, SPACE and FRACTALS

[12] Clarke, Arthur C. (2004) *Fractals: The Colors of Infinity,* DVD.

[13] Pinchbeck, Daniel (2006) *The Return of Quetzalcoatl*, p.97.

[14] Penrose, Roger, and Vahe Gurzayan (2011) *Cycles of Time: An Extraordinary New View of the Universe.*

[15] Braden, Gregg (2009) *Fractal Time,* p.27.

[16] Hellinger, Bert and Gabriele ten Hovel (1999) *Acknowledging what Is: Conversations with Bert Hellinger,* p.62.

[17] *Ibid.* p.65.

[18] Stack, Megan, K. (April 11, 2010) "For Poland, plane crash in Russia rips open old wounds", *Los Angeles Times,* http://articles.latimes/2010/apr/world/la-fg-polish-president.

[19] Cienciala, Anna M. *et.al.* Ed. (*Katyn: A Crime Without Punishment, p.2.*

[20] A.O. Scott (February 18, 2009) *Wajda, Andrzej: Katyn,* movie review, "Bearing Witness to Poland's Pain",*N.Y. Times.*

[21] Paul, Allen (1991) *Katyn: Stalin's Massacre and the Triumph of Truth, pp223-237.* See also Snyder, Timothy (2010) *Bloodlands: Europe between Hitler and Stalin,* p.287.

[22] Crozier, Brian (April 30, 2000) "Remembering Katyn", *Hoover Digest,* 2000, No.2, Hoover Institution, Stanford University, Palo Alto, California .Also: *Katyn forest Massacre: Polish deaths at Soviet hands: Doing justice to the dead,* a web site set up by David Paterson Mirams which contains a wealth of information in English, Polish and Russian, including video interviews with former Soviet military who participated in the massacre at Katyn and other sites. While Mr. Mirams continues to maintain that events surrounding of the 2010 plane crash can be explained by co-incidence, I am nevertheless grateful for his assistance in my own research. http://katyn.org.au/dead.html.

[23] Puhl, Jan (January 19, 2011) "Poland Says Russia Shares Blame for Kaczynski Crash", *Der Spiegel Online.*

[24] Shuster, Simon (April, 10, 2010) "Plane Crash Kills Polish President: A Blow to Russian-Poland Relations", *Time Magazine,* www.time.com.

[25] (April 10, 2010) http://www.kavkazcenter.com/eng/cont/22/11899.shtmi.

[26] *Letter from Poland* (April 10, 2010) Tagenlicht. Nl.

[27] Pasek, Beata (April 10, 2010) "Poland Mourns a Devastating Plane Crash " *Time World,* www.time.com/time.world.

[28] *Ibid*.

[29] Kk/pg (November 15,2010) " Opposition calls for U.S. help in Smolensk crash", *The News, Poland,* www.thenews.pl.international

[30] Manne, Joy (June, 2011) "Conceptual Constellations: The History of Nations, Cultures and Religions", *The Knowing Field: International Constellations Journal,* Issue 18, Somerset, England. pp.32-43.

[31] *Ibid*.

[32] Stolley, Roger A. "Pearl Harbor Attack No Surprise" *The Journal of Historical Review, Vol.12, No.1, pp.119-121.*

[33] Mitchell, Greg and Robert J. Lifton (1995) *Hiroshima in America,* pp. 119-121.

[34] *Ibid*.

[35] *Ibid. p.15.*

[36] Lifton, Robert J. (1967) *Death in Life: Survivors of Hiroshima,* p.20 ff.

[37] Freeman, Robert (August 6, 2005) "Was the Atomic Bombing of Japan Necessary?" *Common Dreams,* www.commondreams.org/views06/0806-25htm.

[38] Mitchell, *op.cit.* p.224

[39] *Ibid. pp.* 3-7.

[40] *Ibid.* pp. 17-18.

[41] Fulbright, J. William (1966) *The Arrogance of Power.*

[42] Dower, John (1999) *Embracing Defeat: Japan in the Wake of World War II,* p.64.

[43] Lifton, *op.cit.* p.81.

[44] Oe, Kenzaburo (September27, 2011) "Resignation to and responsibility for Fukushima disaster", Speech given at Tokyo anti-nuclear rally, 9/19/2011, http://criticality.org. See also: Hiroko Tabuchi (2004) *Godzilla on My Mind: Fifty Years of the King of Monsters.*

[45] Osnos, Evan (March 28, 2011) "Aftershocks", *The New Yorker,* www.newyorker.com/2011/03/28/110.

[46] De Borbon, Antonio (March 15, 2011) "The nightmare returns: Chilling echoes of Hiroshima in images of aftermath of tsunami", *The Daily Mail,* www.co.uk/news/article-1366126/japan.

[47] *Ibid.* I feel that it is also important to note that the world-wide alternative media has expressed serious doubts that this extraordinary earthquake/tsunami was a natural event. Motives and methods for an attack on Japan are open to speculation and I do not feel qualified to offer further comment.

[48] Kaku, Michio (March, 18, 2011) foxnewsinsider.com.

[49] Nimmo, Kurt (November, 22, 2011) "Mass Hydrovolcanic Explosion Inevitable at Fukushima", www.infowars.com.

[50] Norris, Viviane (May, 17, 2011) "Interview with Akira Tokuhiro, Nuclear Engineer: Fukushima and the Mass Media", www.huffingtonpost.com.

TRAUMA: TIME, SPACE and FRACTALS

[51] Shimatsu, Yoichi (December 6, 2011) "The Death of the Pacific Ocean: Fukushima Debris Soon to Hit American Shores", www.rense.com.

[52] *Ibid.*

[53] Arudo, Debito (November, 2011) " The costly fallout of *tatemae* and Japan's culture of deceit", www.japantimes.co.jp.

[54] Yablokov, Alexey, *et.al.* (2009) *Chernobyl: Consequences of the Catastrophe for People and the Environment.* See also: Busby, Chris (1995) *Wings of Death,* Petryna, Adriana (2002) *Life Exposed: Biological Citizens after Chernobyl,* and Caldicott, Helen, (December 2, 2011) "After Fukushima: Enough is Enough", www.nytimes.com.

[55] Debito, *loc.cit.*

[56] Shimatsu, Yoichi (April 12, 2011) "Secret Weapons Program Inside Fukushima", www.globalresearch.ca.

[57] Frackler, Martin (September 9, 2011) "Fukushima's Long Link to a Dark Nuclear Past " www.nytimes.com. Also: http://anngwyn.wisrville.org/2011/09/12.

[58] Shimatsu (April 12, 2011) *loc. cit.*

[59] Pastreich, Emmanuel (July 19, 2011) Translation of Haruki Murakami's Speech at Barcelona in "Japan Focus", *Korea Circles and Squares,* http://circlesandsquares.asia.

[60] Osnos, Evan (October 17, 2011) "Letter from Fukushima: The Fallout", www.newyorker.com.

[61] Osnos, Evan (March 28, 2011) "Aftershocks", www.newyorker.com.

[62] Ichikawa, Keiko (August 28, 2011) "A Letter from Fukushima: Severely malformed babies have been killed in Japan", *Australian Cannonball Nuclear News,* http:Australian.cannonball.com.

TRAUMA: TIME, SPACE and FRACTALS

[63] Slodkowski, Antoni and Yuriko Nakao (April 19, 2011) "Sunflowers melt Fukushima's nuclear snow" www.reuters.com.

[64] Williams, Terry Tempest (May 15, 1995) "We Are All *Hibakusha*: A 'Downwinder' in Hiroshima, *The Nation Magazine,* pp.661-666.

[65] Mitchell, Greg and Lifton, Robert J. (1995) *Hiroshima in America: A Half Century of Denial*, p.13, and Greene, Gayle Jacoba (1999) *The Women Who Knew Too Much.*

[66] Bryson, Bill (2006) *The Life and Times of The Thunderbolt Kid,* p.73.

[67] *Ibid,* pp.122-23.

[68] Medved, Harry and David (1984) *The Hollywood Hall of Shame,* pp.47-52.

[69] Wasserman, Harvey (1962) *Killing Our Own,* pp. 58-64.

[70] Williams, Terry Tempest *The Clan of One-Breasted Women* (1991) p.281ff.

[71] *Ibid.*

[72] Rosenberg, Howard L. (1980) *Atomic Soldiers: American Victims of Nuclear Experiments.* See also: Fradkin, Philip L. (1989) *Fallout: An American Nuclear Tragedy.*

[73] Smokler, Kevin (winter2009/2010) "This Associative Life: An Interview with Terry Tempest Williams", *Rain Taxi Review of Books,* www.coyoteclan.com.

[74] *Refuge, op.cit.* p.90

[75] Williams, Terry Tempest (May 15, 1995) "We Are All Hibakusha: A 'Downwinder' in Hiroshima", *The Nation,* pp.661-121.

[76] Foote, Shelby (1986) *The Civil War: A Narrative.* See also Catton, Bruce, (1988) *Civil War, Vols. 1-111.*

TRAUMA: TIME, SPACE and FRACTALS

[77] Woodard, Colin (2011) *American Nations: A History of Eleven Rival Regional Cultures of North America,* pp-65-72.

[78] *Ibid.* pp. 82-91.

[79] Drockton, Paul (June 2011) "Gone with the Wind", www.moneyteachers.org.

[80] Roberts, Blain and Ethan J. Kytle (December 22, 2010) "Dancing around History", *The New York Times,* http://opininator.blogs.

[81] *Ibid,* and Seeyle, Katherine O. (November 30, 2010) "Celebrating Secession Without slaves", www.nytimes.com.

[82] Doyle, Leonard (February 21, 2009) "America Unmasked: the Ku Klux Klan is Alive and Kicking in 2009", *UK Independent* and www.powerhousbooks.com and O,Donnell, Patrick,(Ed.)(2006) *The Ku Klux Klan: Rebirth of the Society of Blood and Death.*

[83] Jensen, Robert (2005) *The Heart of Whiteness: Confronting Racism and White Privilege.*

[84] Potok, Mark (June 11, 2008) "President Obama? Many White Supremacists are Celebrating", www.spl.org.

[85] Nisbett, Richard and Dov Cohen (1996) *Culture of Honor: The Psychology of Violence in the South.*

[86] Bryson, Bill (2006) *The Life and Times of the Thunderbolt Kid,* p.119.

[87] Nisbett, *loc.cit.*

[88] Birkenhead, Peter (December 27, 2011) "Why we still can't talk about slavery", www.salon,com.

[89] Hartman, Thom (2011) "The True Story of the Boston Tea Party", *The Thom Hartman Reader,* pp.266-273.

TRAUMA: TIME, SPACE and FRACTALS

[90] Holland, Joshua (September 16, 2011) " Has American Style Conservatism Become a Religion?", www.alternet.com

[91] Moran, Lee (December, 12, 2011) *The Daily Mail,* www.dailymail.co.uk.

[92] Wolf, Naomi (November 2, 2011) www.peacenews,org.

[93] Jensen, Robert (September 9, 2011) "Imperial Delusions", www.commondreams.org.

[94] Stan, Adele (September 16, 2011) www.alternet.org, and Johnson, Ben (October 2, 2011) "Rick Perry's Hunting Camp Called 'Niggerhead'", www.slate.com. Also: Lafantasie, Glenn (December 10, 2010) "How the South rationalizes secession", www.salon.com.

[95] Birkenhead, Peter (December 27, 2011) "Why we still can't talk about slavery", www.salon.com.

[96] Cook, Robert J. (2007) *The American Civil War Centennial, 1961-1965: Making the Modern South.*

[97] Birkenhead, *loc. cit.* and Lundberg, James (June 8, 2011) "Thanks A Lot, Ken Burns", www.dallasnews.com. The Mason Dixon line formed a cultural and geographical boundary between the Northeastern states and the slave-holding South and those regions are stilled called "Dixie".

[98] Cook, *loc. cit.*

[99] Horvitz, Tony (1998) *Confederates in the Attic,* pp.7-8, 16.

[100] *Ibid* p.209.

[101] Lafantasie, Glenn, (September 14, 2011) "The foolishness of Civil War re-enactors", www.salon.com.

[102] Parramore, Lynn (December 30, 2011) "What You Didn't Know about the South: Surprises From a White Southerner, www.alternet.org.

[103] Lafantasie, *op.cit.* Seealso: Orr, Tim (May 18, 2011) "Reconsidering Civil War re-enactors in the sesquicentennial or the insight and foolishness of Glenn LaFantasie", *The People's Contest:A Civil War Era Digital Arching Project,* www.psu.edu/dept/richardscenter/2011/05/reconsidering-civil-war-re-enactors.

[104] *Ibid.*

TRAUMA: TIME, SPACE and FRACTALS

BIBLIOGRAPHY

Allison, Fiona (September 21, 2009) "The Katyn Forest Massacre of 1940: The Implications of its Discovery in 1943", www.suite101.com/content/the-katyn-forest-massacre-of-1943.

Arguelles, Jose (2002) *Time and the Technosphere: The Law of Time and Human Affairs,* Bear and Co., Rochester, Vermont.

Arima, Tetsuo (2008) *Nuclear Power, Shoriki and the CIA,* Shinchosha, in Japanese.

Arudou, Debito (November 1, 2011) "The costly fallout of *tatemae* and Japan's culture of deceit", *The Japan Times,* www.japantimes.co.jp/text/fl20111101ad.html.

Babich, Dmitry (March 7, 2010) "Poland: Putin's speech won't please everyone". http://en.rian.ru/analysis.20100407/158473805.html.

Barry, Ellen, Nicholas Kulish and Michael Piotrowski, "Polish President Dies in Jet Crash in Russia", *NYTimes.com,* www.nytimes.com/2010/04/11/world/Europe/11poland.html.

Birkenhead, Peter (December 27, 2011) "Why we still can't talk about slavery", www.salon.com/2011/12/27/why_we_still_cant_talk_about_slavery.

Braden, Gregg (2009) *Fractal Time,* Hay House, Inc. Carlsbad, California.

Bryson, Bill (2006) *The Life and Times of the Thunderbolt Kid,* Broadway Books, NYC.

Busby, Chris (1995) *Wings of Death: Nuclear Pollution and Human Health,* Green Audit Books, Aberystwyth, Wales.

Caldicott, Helen (December 2, 2011) "After Fukushima: Enough is Enough", www.nytimes.com.

Calleman, Carl Johan (2009) *The Purposeful Universe,* Bear and Co. Rochester, Vermont.

TRAUMA: TIME, SPACE and FRACTALS

_____, (August 19, 2009) "The Tortuguero Monument 6 and the Mayan End Date", www.calleman.com/content/articles/the_tortuguero%20_monument.htm.

_____ (2004) *The Mayan Calendar and the Transformation of Consciousness,* Bear and Company, Rochester, Vermont.

Catton, Bruce (1988) *Civil War,* Vols. I-III (1951-1953) Random House, NYC.

Celente, Gerald, *Trends Research Institute,* www.geraldcelente.com .

Cienciala, Anna M. et.al. ed. (2007) *Katyn: A Crime Without Punishment,* Yale University Press, New Haven, Connecticut.

Clarke, Arthur C. (2004) *Fractals: The Colors of Infinity,* DVD.

Coe, M.D. (1999) *The Maya,* Thames and Hudson, 6th ed. NYC.

--------------- (1994) *Mexico; From the Olmecs to the Aztecs,* 4th ed. Thames and Hudson, NYC.

Cook, Robert J. (2007) *Commemoration: The American Civil War Centennial, 1961-65: Making the Modern South,* Louisiana State University Press, Baton Rouge, Louisiana.

Cornwell, Rupert (December 20, 2010) "After 150 years, the Civil War still divides the United States" *The Independent,* www.independent.co.uk/opinion/commentators/rupert-cor.

Crozier, Brian (April 30, 2000) "Remembering Katyn" *Hoover Institution,* Stanford University, *Hoover Digest* 2000,No.2, www.hoover.org/publications/hoover-digest/article/6489.

Doyle, Leonard (February 21, 2009) "America Unmasked: The images that reveal the Ku Klux Klan is alive and kicking in 2009", *U.K. Independent* and www.powerhousebooks.com.

TRAUMA: TIME, SPACE and FRACTALS

Dower, John (1999) *Embracing Defeat: Japan in the Wake of World War II*, W.W. Norton and Company, NYC.

Drockton, Paul (June 2011) "Gone With the Wind", www.moneyteachers.org/Trouble.html.

ENENEWS ADMIN (December 28, 2011) " UN Agency: Reactor 3 exploded a second time 24 hours later – then wind and rain brought high levels of radiation over Tokyo, Sendai, Nagano, *World Meteorological Organization*, http://enenews.com/un-agency-ractor-3-exploded-a-second-time.

Flood, Alison (June 13, 2011) "Murakami laments Japan's nuclear policy", *UK Guardian:* http://www.ukguardian.co.uk/books/2011/jun/13/murakami-japan-nuclear-policy.

Foote, Shelby (1986) *The Civil War : A Narrative, Vols. I-III*. Vintage Books, NYC.

Frackler, Martin (September 9,2011) "Fukushima's Long Link to a Dark Nuclear Past", www.nytimes.com. Also: St. Just, A., "Japan and the History of Place", http://anngwyn.wisrville.org/2011/09/12.

Fradkin, Philip L. (1989) *Fallout: An American Nuclear Tragedy*, University of Arizona Press, Tucson, Arizona.

Freeman, Robert (August 6, 2005) "Was the Atomic Bombing of Japan Necessary?" *Common Dreams*, www.commondreams,org/views06/0806-25htm.

Galeano, Eduardo (1973) *Open Veins of Latin America*, Monthly Review Press, NYC.

Grossinger, Richard (2010) *2013: Raising the Earth to the Next Vibration* , North Atlantic Books, Berkeley, California.

Hadden, Robert Lee (1999) *Reliving the Civil War: A Re-enactor's Handbook*, Stackpole Books, Mechanicsberg, Pennsylvania.

TRAUMA: TIME, SPACE and FRACTALS

Hartman, Thom (2011) *The Thom Hartman Reader,* Berrett-Koehler Publishers,Inc., San Francisco, California.

Hawking, Stephen (1998) *A Brief History of Time,* Bantam, NYC.

He, Biyu Jade, et.al. (May 13, 2010) "The temporal, structural and functional significance of scale free brain activity" *Neuron,* Vol. 66, Issue 3, 353-369.

Hellinger, Bert and Gabriele ten Hovel (1999) *Acknowledging What Is: Conversations with Bert Hellinger,* Zeig Tucker and Company, Inc., Phoenix, Arizona.

Hellinger, Bert (2008) *Together in the Shadow of God,* Hellinger Publications, Berchtesgaden, Germany.

Hersey, John, (1946) *Hiroshima,* Random House, NYC.

Holland, Joshua, (September 16, 2011) "*Has American-Style Conservatism Become a Religion?*", http://www.alternet.org/story/152434/has_american-style_conservatism_become_a_religion.

Horwitz, Tony (1998) *Confederates in the Attic: Dispatches From the Unfinished Civil War:* Vintage Books, NYC.

Ichikawa, Keiko (August 28, 2011) *A Letter from Fukushima,* "Severely malformed babies have been killed in Japan", Australian Cannonball Nuclear News: http://australiancannonball.com/2011/08/severely-malformed-babies-have-been-killed-...

Jenkins, John Major (2009) *The 2012 Story: The Myths, Fallacies, and Truth Behind the Most Intriguing Dates in History,* Jeremy Tarcher, NYC.

Jensen, Robert (2005) *The Heart of Whiteness: Confronting Racism and White Privilege,* City Lights, San Francisco, California.

_____ (September 9, 2011) "*Imperial Delusions*", www.commondreams.org/view/2011/09/09-15.

Johnson, Ben (October 2, 2011) "Rick Perry's Hunting Camp Called Niggerhead", www.slate,com.

TRAUMA: TIME, SPACE and FRACTALS

Jungk, Robert, (1958) *Brighter Than a Thousands Suns,* Houghton Mifflin, Harcourt, Brace, Boston, Massachusetts.

Kavkaz Center Monitor (April 11, 2010) "Georgian TV foretold murder of Polish President by Russian KGB terrorists" www.kavkazcenter.com/eng/content/2010/04/11/11838.sht.

Kobayashi, Chetna, (June, 2011) "A Journey to Okinawa, Hiroshima and Nagasaki", *The Knowing Field: International Constellations Journal,* Issue 18, Somerset, England.

Lafantasie, Glenn W. (12/20/2010) *"How the South rationalizes secession",* Salon; War Room:www.salon.com/news/politics/war/_room/2010/12/19

_____(9/14/2011) *"The foolishness of Civil War re-enactors",* Salon/War Room: www.salon.com/news/politics/war_room/2011/05/08/civil_war_sesquicentennial

Leary, Joy Degruy (2005) *Post-Traumatic Slave Syndrome,* Uptone Press, Milwaukie. Oregon.

Leopold, Les (October 23, 2011) "The Shocking Graphic Data that Shows Exactly What Motivates the Occupy Movement" www.Alternet.com.

_____(1967) *Death in Life: Survivors of Hiroshima,* Random House, NYC.

Lukacher, Ned (1998) *Time-Fetishes: The Secret History of Eternal Recurrence,* Duke University Press, Durham, North Carolina.

Lundberg, James M. (June 8, 2011) "Thanks a Lot, Ken Burns", www.dallasnews.com/opinion/Sunday-commentary/2011.

Lungold, Ian Xel, (February 17, 2004) *Welcome to the Evolution: Solving the Mystery of the Mayan Calendar,* UFO TV: DVD, White Horse, Canada.

Mann, Charles C. (2005) *1491: New Revelations of the Americas before Columbus,* Vintage Books, NYC.

Manne, Joy, (June 2011) "Conceptual Constellations: The History of Nations, Cultures and Religions", *The Knowing Field: International Constellations Journal,* Issue 18, Somerset, England, pp.32-43.

McElvaine, Robert (1/15/2011) "Still fighting against our own cause," *Politico* http://www.politico.com/news/stories/0111/47498_Page 2.html.

Mc Kenna, Terence (1994) *True Hallucinations,* Harper Collins, NYC.

Mc Pherson, James, M. (2003) *Battle Cry of Freedom: The Civil War Era,* Oxford University Press, Oxford, England.

Medved, Harry and Michael (1984) *The Hollywood Hall of Shame,* Perigee Books, NYC.

Mirams, David Paterson (1991) *Katyn Forest Massacre: Polish Deaths at Soviet Hands: Doing justice to the dead,* http://katyn.org.au.dead.html.

Mitchell, Greg, and Robert Jay Lifton (1995) *Hiroshima in America: A Half Century of Denial,* Avon books, NYC.

Moran, Lee (December 12, 2011) "Half-black, half-white and almost everything it does stinks" *The Daily Mail* ,www.dailymail.co.uk/article-2073094.

Murakami, Haruki (April 10, 2001) *Underground: The Tokyo Gas Attack and the Japanese Psyche,* Vintage, NYC.

_____ (May 2003) *After the Quake: Stories,* Vintage, NYC.

Nimmo, Kurt (November 22, 2011) "Massive Hydrovolcanic Explosion Inevitable at Fukushima", www.infowars.com.

Nisbett, Richard, and Dov Cohen (1996) *Culture of Honor: The Psychology of Violence in the South,* Westview Press, Boulder, Colorado.

Norris, Fran H. (November 2001) "Trauma and PTSD in Japan" *PTSD Research Quarterly,* Vol. 22/No. 3.ISSN:1050-1835:http://www.ptsd.va.gov.

TRAUMA: TIME, SPACE and FRACTALS

Norris, Vivian (May 17, 2011) "Interview with Akira Tokuhiro, Nuclear Engineer: Fukushima and the Mass Media", www.huffingtonpost.com.

O'Donnell, Patrick, Ed. (2006) *Ku Klux Klan: The Rebirth of the Society of Blood and Death,* Idea Man Productions, West Orange, New Jersey.

Orr, Tim (May 18, 2011) "Reconsidering Civil War re-enactors in the sesquicentennial or the insight and foolishness of Glenn LaFantasie". *The People's Contest: A Civil War Era Digital Archiving Project,* www.psu.edu/dept/richardscenter/2011/05/.

Osnos, Evan (March 28, 2011) "Aftershocks", *The New Yorker,* www.newyorker.com/2011/03/28/110.

_____, (October 17, 2011) "Letter from Fukushima: The Fallout", *The New Yorker,* www.newyorker.com/2011/10/17/110.

Parramore, Lynn (December 30, 2011) "What you Didn't Know About the South: Surprises from a White Southerner", www.AlterNet.com.

Pasek, Beata (April 10, 2010) "Poland Mourns a Devastating Plane Crash" *TIME World,* www.time.com/time/world/article/o,8599,1981075,00.html.

Pastreich, Emmanuel (July 19, 2011) "Translation of Murakami Haruki's Speech at Barcelona in *Japan Focus, Korea Circles and Squares,*http://circlesandsquares.asia/2011/07/19/translation-of-murakami-harukis-speech-at-barcelona.

Paul, Allen (1991) *Katyn: Stalin's Massacre and the Triumph of Truth,* Charles Scribner and Sons, NYC.

Penrose, Roger, and Vahe Gurzadyan (2011) *Cycles of Time: An Extraordinary New View of the Universe,* Alfred A. Knopf Inc., NYC.

Petryna, Adriana (2002) *Life Exposed: Biological Citizens After Chernobyl,* Princeton University Press, Princeton, New Jersey.

Pinchbeck, Daniel (2006) *The Return of Quetzalcoatl,* Jeremy Tarcher, NYC.

Puhl, Jan 9 (January 19, 2011) "Poland Says Russia Shares Blame for Kaczynski Crash" *Der Speigel Online International*,www.spiegel.de/international/Europe/o,1518.740347,00.html.

Roberts, Blain and Ethan J. Kytle (December 22, 2010) "Dancing Around History". *The New York Times*, http://opinionator.blogs.nytimes.com/2010/12/21.

Potok, Mark, (June 11, 2008) "President Obama? Many White Supremacists are Celebrating", *Southern Poverty Law Center*, http://www.splcenter.org/blog/2008/06/11.

Rosenberg, Howard L. (1980) *Atomic Soldiers: American Victims of Nuclear Experiments,* Beacon Press, Boston, Massachusetts..

Schearer, Tony (1971) *Lord of the Dawn,* Naturegraph Publishers, Happy Camp, California.

Schele, Linda and David Freidel (1990) *A Forest of Kings: The Untold Story of the Ancient Maya,* William Morrow and Co. NYC.

Scott, A.O. (February 18, 2009) *"Katyn 2007:* Bearing Witness to Poland's Pain", http://movies.nytimes.com/2009/02/18movies/18katy.html.

Seeyle, Katharine O. (November 30, 2010) "Celebrating Secession without the Slaves", *The New York Times*,www.nytimes.com/2010/11/30.

Selbie, Joseph and David Steinmetz (2011) *The Yugas: Keys to Understanding Our Hidden Past and Future Enlightenment,* Crystal Clarity Publishers, Nevada City, California.

Shimatsu, Yoichi (April 12, 2011) "Secret Weapons Program Inside Fukushima" *Global Research,* www.globalresearch.ca/index.php?aid=24275&context=va.

_____ (October 12, 2011) "The Fukushima Disaster: What Happened on Day One", *Global Research,* www.globalresearch.ca/index.php?aid=24275&context=va.

_____(December 6, 2011) "The Death of the Pacific Ocean: Fukushima Debris Soon to Hit American Shores", www.rense.com/general95/death.htm.

Shuster, Simon (April 10, 2010) "Plane Crash Kills Polish President: A Blow to Russian-Poland Relations", www.time.com/time/world/article/0,8599,1981060,oo.html.

Smokler, Kevin, (Winter 2009/2010) "This Associative Life: An Interview with Terry Tempest Williams", *Rain Taxi Review of Books,* www.coyoteclan.com.

Snyder, Timothy (2010) *Bloodlands: Europe between Hitler and Stalin,* Basic Books, NYC.

Sobczyk, Marcin (May 25, 2010) " Russian Dissidents Say Poland 'Naïve' on Plane Crash Investigation", *New Europe,* http://blogs.wsj.com/new-europe/2010/05/25.

Stack, Megan K. (April 11, 2010) "For Poland, plane crash in Russia rips open old wounds, *Los Angeles Times,*http://latimes.com/2010/apr11/world/la-fg-polish-president.

Stan, Adele (September 16, 2011) "*Would a Perry v. Obama Contest Be a Confederacy v. Union Rematch?*" www.alternet.org.

Stray, Geoff (2005) *Beyond 2012: Catastrophe and Awakening,* Bear and Co. Rochester, Vermont

Stephens, John Lloyd, and Frederick Catherwood (1841) *Incidents of Travel in Central America, Chiapas and Yucatan,* Harper and Brothers, NYC. Reprint: Dover Publications, 1969.

Stolley, Roger A. "Pearl Harbor Attack No Surprise", *The Journal of Historical Review,* Vol.12, No.1,pp.119,121.

Swanson, David (2010) *War is a Lie,* Charlottesville, Virginia.

_____, (August 5, 2011) " Truman Lied, Hundreds of Thousands Died" www.opednews.com.

TRAUMA: TIME, SPACE and FRACTALS

Tabuchi, Hiroko (October 14, 2011) "Citizen's Testing Finds 20 Hot Spots Around Tokyo" www.nytimes/2011/10/15.

Tsutsui, William (2004) *Godzilla on My Mind: Fifty Years of the King of Monsters*, Palgrave Macmillan, NYC.

Von Hagen, Victor Wolfgang (1990) *Mayan Explorer: John Lloyd Stephens and the Lost Cities of Central America and Yucatan*, Chronicle Books, San Francisco, California.

Walsh, Joan (June 9, 2011) "*Everything You know About the Civil War is Wrong*" www.salon.com/print.html?URL=/opinion/walsh/politics/2...6/10/2011.

Ward, Geoffrey C., Rick Burns and Ken Burns, (1992) *The Civil War: An Illustrated History*, Alfred A. Knopf Inc. NYC.

Wasserman, Harvey, (1982) *Killing Our Own: The Disaster of America's Experience of Atomic Radiation*, Delacorte Press, NYC.

Williams, Terry Tempest (January 1990) "The Clan of One Breasted Women" *Northern Lights Magazine*, Missoula, Montana, Volume VI, No 1.

_____ (May 15, 1995) " We Are All *Hibakusha*: A 'Downwinder' in Hiroshima, *The Nation*, pp. 661-666.

_____ (2001) Second Edition, *Refuge: An Unnatural History of Family and Place*, Vintage Books, NYC.

Wilson, Peter (2011) *The Thirty Years War: Europe's Tragedy*, Harvard University Press, Cambridge, Massachusetts.

Wolf, Naomi (November 2, 2011) "We May Be Witnessing the First Large Global Conflict Where People Are Aligned by Consciousness and Not Nation State or Religion" www.peacenews.org.

Woodard, Colin (2011) *American Nations: A History of Eleven Rival Regional Cultures of North America*, Viking Penguin, NYC.

Yablokov, Alexey, et.al. (2009) *Chernobyl: Consequences of the Catastrophe for People and the Environment*, New York Academy of Sciences.

Made in the USA
San Bernardino, CA
15 November 2016